P9-DOG-508

To

MARIKA DANIELLE MOORE

From

BRIAN ALLSOPP   DAVID TSHINE SECHABA

ERNA ALLSOPP

Date

18 MAY 2007

A Taste of the Spirit

© 2006 Christian Art Gifts, RSA
     Christian Art Gifts Inc., IL, USA

Designed by Christian Art Gifts

Printed in China

ISBN 978-1-86920-676-5

07 08 09 10 11 12 13 14 15 – 11 10 9 8 7 6 5 4 3

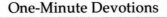

One-Minute Devotions

A TASTE
OF THE
Spirit

KAREN MOORE

✝ christian
art gifts®

Introduction

Fresh fruit is essential if we want to stay healthy. It nourishes the body, renews our energy levels and is a delight to the taste buds and the eye. God offers us 'fruit' so that we can stay healthy in spirit. This fruit nourishes the soul. Peeling off layers of emotions, ideas, and information that bombards our senses every day from everywhere, can make it difficult to get to the sweet fruit of peace, patience and gentleness. Some days, we're not even sure whether these things are even attainable.

As it turns out, we're all in this together, all gatherers of the harvest of God's goodness. A little inspiration, enlightenment and wholesome fruit to put in our baskets can make the journey a little bit easier. Galatians 5:22-23 has been a favorite fruit for generations of readers. Let's see if there's anything we might have missed among its basket of virtues.

We rejoice in our loving and generous Creator who planted the seeds of hope within us so we can all reap from His bounty. It is only through Him that we can receive a full taste of the Spirit.

~ *Karen Moore*

January

Creating a New Spirit

The fruit of the Spirit is love, joy, peace, patience, kindness, goodness, faithfulness, gentleness and self-control. Against such things there is no law.
Galatians 5:22-23

When a new year begins, we make promises to ourselves and to God to live better lives. We promise we'll pray more, love more, or give more to those around us. God always hears those promises and blesses the spirit in which we make them. He knows that right at that moment, we really mean to follow through.

Perhaps this year, if we seek more of His Spirit to help us keep those promises, we really will do it. Let's start together, asking for a clean heart and a new way to share His love.

A Taste of Joy

As I open the door to the new year, Lord, strengthen and renew my joy, my love and my commitment to You. With every beat of my heart, let me seek Your will every day. Amen.

In the Spirit of Love

*Be imitators of God, therefore, as dearly
loved children and live a life of love, just
as Christ loved us and gave Himself up for us
as a fragrant offering and sacrifice to God.*
Ephesians 5:1-2

Have you ever watched young children as they
play? They sometimes pretend to play the guitar
like Daddy, or pretend to bake a cake like Mommy.
Children are great at imitating the people closest to
them. They want very much to be like the ones they
love.

In Ephesians, Paul says that as we develop a
spirit of love, we should try to imitate Jesus. Because He is someone we love and want to be close
to, it should be easy to do. In fact, it should be fun,
almost child's play. As you put on a spirit of love
today, see if you can imitate Jesus and be like Him
in some special way. If your heart is sincere, Jesus
will surely be pleased.

A Taste of the Spirit
Lord, help me to have a childlike faith in You today,
imitating Your love for others, creating a spirit of peace
within my soul. Bless this day. Amen.

Love Is an Action Word

*Dear children, let us not love with words
or tongue but with actions and in truth.*
1 John 3:18

How do we understand the word *love*? What would love in action feel like, taste like, or smell like? How can we know if we are sharing love in action and in truth?

Think about yesterday. Consider every interaction you had with your spouse, a co-worker, a child, or a neighbor and run it through your mind on instant replay. Did that interaction create closeness, a sense of well-being, a moment shared that left you both feeling better for it? Actions created in love feel good. They lift our spirits and encourage our hearts.

God is love because He sent Jesus to redeem us. You are love when you fit your words and your actions together for His glory.

A Taste of Love

Lord, let me radiate love to everyone I meet today. Let me lift the spirits of others and strengthen their hearts in all that I do. Amen.

The Apple of His Eye

*For the L*ORD*'s portion is His people, Jacob His*
allotted inheritance. He shielded him and cared
for him; He guarded him as the apple of His eye.
Deuteronomy 32:9-10

When you're the apple of someone's eye you feel
pretty special. Perhaps you were the apple of your
grandmother's eye, or your Aunt Mary's. Perhaps
you have someone in your life who is the apple of
your eye. What a delightful position to be in!

Imagine being the apple of God's eye. Jacob was
shielded and cared for. He was guarded and protected. What joy it is to know that we are cared for
in the same way. We are shielded from things we
don't even know God protected us from. We are
cared for by angels with tender mercy all through
the day. Why? Because we're loved so much. Remember today, wherever you go, that you are the
apple of God's eye.

A Taste of the Spirit
Lord, let me act today as the apple of Your eye. Let me
know Your protection, mercy and love in all that comes
my way. Amen.

How Do You Quench Love?

Many waters cannot quench love;
rivers cannot wash it away.
Song of Solomon 8:7

One of the most passionate messages in the Bible says that love cannot be quenched. What does that mean? Typically, we might think that we could quench a thirst by drinking water, or quench a feeling by subduing it. However, if rivers cannot wash love away or waters quench it then love is here to stay.

God's love for us is unquenchable. The love you have for someone else may feel that way too. You may think that nothing can change it and that you will always want more of it. Will your love change or dry up? Will your love continue to flow, flooding the heart of your beloved with every breath? If so, you'll experience the flavor of God's love for you.

Promise those who are dearest to you that nothing will quench your love for them either.

A Taste of Love

Lord, let me overflow with love today, drinking You in, breathing You out so that everyone will see more of You, less of me and feel Your unquenchable love. Amen.

Loving the Unlovable

"Love your enemies, do good to those who hate you,
bless those who curse you, pray for those who mistreat
you. Do to others as you would have them do to you."
Luke 6:27-28, 31

It only seems right to love the people you care about, but to love your enemies? Isn't that going just a bit too far? "Pray for those who mistreat you?" Well, that's a nice idea, but can we do it? We treat others with compassion and kindness because we expect to be treated with compassion and kindness in return.

What happens when we treat others with kindness, but they throw blame at us or tell lies about us? What happens when even friends betray us? The answer seems pretty clear, "Love, do good, bless, and pray." The abusive actions of others are no excuse for us to be abusive in return. They are opportunities for us to put Jesus into action, for us to show God's love, even if we can't quite show our own.

A Taste of Love
Lord, let me love all those around me today. Let me be an example of Your care, Your gifts and Your presence wherever I am. Amen.

Sing for Joy!

Let all who take refuge in You be glad; let them
ever sing for joy. Spread Your protection over them,
that those who love Your name may rejoice in You.
Psalm 5:11

Think joy! Sing joy! Live joy! There's something different in a day spent in joy – something memorable happens. Joyful days stand out because they are rare ... they are an oasis from the normal way we do things.

Imagine what it would be like if you decided to rise every morning, rejoicing in the Lord, singing for joy, living in peace because you knew without a doubt that you are protected and loved. You know that the Lord protects you like the wings of an angel gently wrapped around your shoulders.

Step into the day with a smile for the world, renewed energy for those you love and a decision in your heart that today you'll do it. Think joy! Sing joy! Live joy!

A Taste of Joy
Lord, I'm walking, I'm singing, I'm running with You all day today in great joy! Thank You for being with me. Amen.

A Happy Heart

A happy heart makes the face cheerful,
but heartache crushes the spirit.
Proverbs 15:13

What do you do when your spirit is crushed? How do you find joy again? Do you simply decide to put on a happy face or is there something else that must first happen inside you before that cheerful face can be seen again?

We can acknowledge suffering, but we don't have to dwell on it. It is possible to return fairly quickly to a happy heart. How? Try something like this. Step away from your sorrow and put it outside yourself. Ask Jesus to carry it for you while you go out for a walk.

Open your eyes to the world around you and your heart to others. Talk to a neighbor, reach out to a friend and find a reason to laugh. By the time you return home, the burden you've been feeling will have lifted. Your face will tell you so.

A Taste of Comfort

Lord, help me to realize that my sorrows are important to You and that I don't need to carry them alone. Bless this situation and walk with me until the answers come. Amen.

Joyful, Patient, Faithful ... Me?

*Be joyful in hope, patient in affliction,
faithful in prayer. Share with God's people
who are in need. Practice hospitality.*
Romans 12:12-13

Hope gives wings to the soul. Hope changes the way we perceive the world. It renews the spirit. Indeed, hope gives us reason to rejoice.

When affliction comes and patience is short, we lose hope. Sometimes we even lose our ability or our desire to pray. What do we do then? The writer of Romans gives us a suggestion. When our hope is down, we can turn our attention to others. We can share with God's people in need and practice hospitality. We can take the opportunity to volunteer our services to others and take our minds off our lagging spirits. In doing so, we may discover that hope returns. Giving creates wings of hope.

A Taste of Hope

Lord, renew my hope today. Let my spirit rise as I work, live and serve others in Your name, with the full knowledge that You are the Creator and Source of all hope. Let me hope in You again. Amen.

What Shall I Do with Today?

*This is the day the LORD has made;
let us rejoice and be glad in it.*

Psalm 118:24

Every sunrise brings a choice. We can choose to live in the light of God's love and blessing, or we can choose to crawl back under the covers and go it alone. We can choose to see each person around us as difficult and cruel or we can choose to see each person as someone that the Lord loves and has redeemed. The choice is significant.

This is the day the Lord has made. It was created for you to enjoy now. This day is the one we have to live in and rejoice in. When the sun goes down on this day, will you have spent it in joy? Will you be the reason someone else rejoiced today? You are the light of the world and this is your day to shine.

A Taste of the Light

Lord, as I walk in Your light, help me, with Your love and compassion, to bless each one that crosses my path. Help me to keep choosing to see the good in each person I encounter. Amen.

Living in Harmony

For God is not a God of disorder but of peace.
1 Corinthians 14:33 NLT

Okay, brothers, sisters, family, kids and co-workers, this is your day to make peace with one another. This is your day to live in harmony.

Harmony doesn't mean you all have to sing the same note or even the same song. It just means you have to hum along and keep things running smoothly. That's the way to maintain order in your day. Discord, chaos, apathy and anger are all notes of discontent. They'll keep you keyed up, your anxiety at high pitch and your throat ready to scream.

Clean up the chaos and let harmony return. Let your song burst forth into praise for your God who loves you so.

A Taste of Harmony

Lord, let me seek forgiveness from any that I may have offended today. Let me offer the hand of friendship to those I meet today and live in harmony with Your Spirit and Your purpose for my life. Amen.

Messengers of Peace

How beautiful on the mountains are the feet
of those who bring good news, who proclaim peace,
who bring good tidings, who proclaim salvation,
who say to Zion, "Your God reigns!"

Isaiah 52:7

We live on a planet that spins on information overload. A quick glance at the latest headlines informs us of the latest war and where death and destruction are taking their toll. We become emotionally involved and carry the pain of those war-torn places in the very fiber of our beings. Sometimes this becomes more than we can bear. But then, there is always good news! Peace is declared. People are safe and it is easy to breathe again.

So, what if it is your job to declare good news today? Well, in a way you are a messenger because you can bring good news to your family, your colleagues, your friends, and everyone you meet. You can bring them the good news of God's love.

A Taste of Peace

Lord, we may never experience the peace of nations for more than a moment at a time, but we can know Your peace and carry it with us to deliver to everyone we meet. Help me to deliver Your Good News today. Amen.

Love Truth and Peace

"Therefore love truth and peace."
Zechariah 8:19

"Love truth and peace." Well, that seems easy enough. But if we're going to be part of the truth today, if we're going to love truth today, that might mean there's no room for little "untruths". You know, those quick things we say without thinking, like, "You look so good in purple polka dots," or "I'll pray for you," or "I'll call you."

Indeed, we want our friends to feel good, so we may cover up not liking what they choose to wear, and we really do mean to pray for people even when we forget, and "I'll call you" is just a polite version of procrastination ... at least sometimes. Those little "untruths" sneak into our lives all day long and before we know it any sense of peace, is gone. Peace comes when your heart is sincere and your love is genuine. God has put His truth in your heart and His grace will keep you coming back for more.

A Taste of the Truth

Lord, You know the truth about me, even better than I do. Let me live in that truth and honor my friends with my words and my intentions. Let me seek real truth and peace today. Amen.

Pass the Salt

"Salt is good for seasoning. But if it loses its flavor, how do you make it salty again? You must have the qualities of salt among yourselves and live in peace with each other."

Mark 9:50 NLT

Salt is a popular way to enhance the flavor of nearly any dish. It's so popular in fact, that millions of people have to watch how much salt they actually add to their foods. But what if you added the salt and nothing happened, and your favorite dish remained bland and insipid?

This passage from Mark reminds us that we as Christians are the "salt". We're the spice, the ones who enhance life and flavor it with joy. It's the salt of God's love and of the Holy Spirit that we carry inside our hearts, that helps flavor our lives and those of others as well. The right amount of salt makes a dish more desirable. The right amount of salt in your spirit, makes you a lot more desirable as you share your faith. Come on, don't be bland ... share the salt!

A Taste of Salt

Lord, help me to show Your spirit in ways that flavor the lives of those around me. Amen.

The Fruit of the Spirit is Peace

The wisdom that comes from heaven is first of all pure; then peace-loving, considerate, submissive, full of mercy and good fruit, impartial and sincere. Peacemakers who sow in peace raise a harvest of righteousness.
James 3:17-18

We attribute wisdom to certain special people in the world. Those in political and religious leadership roles are thought to be wise. Solomon was thought to be wise. But what is wisdom? We think of Rhodes scholars or great philosophers as wise because we think wisdom has something to do with intellect and being smart. We strive to be smarter than the next person so we can stay slightly ahead of them.

The wisdom of heaven as it turns out, is all about being considerate and showing mercy and kindness. It's about being peace-loving. Wisdom that brings peace is the wisdom you should pray for. If you sow in peace, you'll harvest the goodness and the wisdom that God intends for you.

A Taste of the Spirit

Lord, grant me the wisdom of a loving heart, kindness to extend to every living soul, and the mercy to realize every day that we all need Your grace. Help me to harvest Your peace. Amen.

Give Me Patience Right Now!

*I wait for the L*ORD*, my soul waits, and in*
His word I put my hope. My soul waits for
*the L*ORD *more than watchmen wait for the morning.*

Psalm 130:5-6

Imagine a lonely watchman waiting through the night for the new day to begin. Imagine those quiet hours as he's struggling to stay awake, planning all the morning activities. The watchman can hardly wait for the dawn to break.

Yet, the psalmist emphasizes that *his* waiting is even greater than that of the watchman. His soul longs for the Lord, living on the Word, passing the time in hope. Most of us are neither like the watchman, nor like the psalmist. We don't have the patience to wait night after night. Jesus' own disciples couldn't wait with Him through that long night in the Garden of Gethsemane. Why do we so quickly grow weary of waiting? We pray for patience, but we want the waiting to be over now. Wait in peace.

A Taste of Patience

Lord, help me to wait in hope with Your Word to feed my soul and Your grace to guide my spirit. Help me to wait and not walk ahead of You today. Amen.

Patience and Understanding

A patient man has great understanding,
but a quick tempered man displays folly.
Proverbs 14:29

Sometimes there's a fine line between understanding and foolishness. The old adage that "patience is a virtue" comes to mind here. The reason for it being a virtue is that it's not easy to achieve.

Go back and think a bit about that last conversation you had with your teenager, or the advice you gave your co-worker, or the way you felt about the delay you experienced out on the highway. For that matter, go back and consider those moments when you're not even able to be patient with yourself.

Understanding or folly? The writer of Galatians understood that patience is a much needed fruit of the Spirit, because it is difficult for us to have patience clearly take root in our souls.

A Taste of Patience
Lord, rescue me from impatience. Help me to be more willing to listen, to seek to understand, and to simply give things time to fall into place as they are meant to. Amen.

Be Patient with Everyone

*Encourage the timid, help the weak, be patient with every-
one. Always try to be kind to each other and to everyone else.*
1 Thessalonians 5:14-15

How would you react in each of the following situations?

* Your spouse loses the car keys just as you need them to get to work.
* You're walking into your office building, your hands are full, but no one helps you get the door even though they can see your dilemma.
* Your mother calls before 7:00 AM on a Saturday morning.
* Your toast burns.

Remember that being patient with everyone ties in nicely with encouraging hearts, strengthening spirits, and showing genuine kindness. Give yourself points for every effort you make today.

A Taste of Patience
Lord, help me to clearly see those times when I could have given a little more than I thought I was receiving. Amen.

Does Anybody Really Know What Time It Is?

*Do not forget this one thing, dear friends: With the Lord
a day is like a thousand years, and a thousand years is like
a day. The Lord is not slow in keeping His promise,
as some understand slowness. He is patient with you.*

2 Peter 3:8-9

Have you ever waited in a long line for something
you really wanted? Maybe you wanted theater tick-
ets, or you were going to ride your favorite roller
coaster at the amusement park. Or maybe you were
simply sitting in traffic that didn't budge and you
could have walked home faster.

We're driven by the clock. We're in a hurry to get
up, get to work, get the job done, get home, feed the
kids, get to the store, get to Bible Study, get to bed
and then start all over again. Whatever it is, we're in
a hurry to get there.

God seems to be saying, "Don't worry and don't
hurry." If we believe that God is in the details of our
lives, then we can afford to be a little more patient.
We can afford to allow for His timing.

A Taste of Time

Lord, remind me that my time is always Yours. Let me
move in the rhythm of Your divine timing for all that
You would have me accomplish today. Amen.

Kindness Matters

Be kind and compassionate to one another,
forgiving each other, just as in Christ God forgave you.
Ephesians 4:32

The writer of Ephesians suggests that kindness and compassion go hand in hand with forgiveness. Kindness matters. Compassion helps. Forgiveness heals.

How different our lives would be if people practiced random acts of compassion, crazy moments of forgiveness and loving handfuls of kindness!

Compassion is one of those words that gets to the heart of the matter quickly. It is only needed when a situation is out of control: too much sorrow, too little money, too much need. We prefer to bestow compassion more than we want to be the recipients of it. But at one time or another we all need to receive kindness, compassion, and forgiveness from someone else.

A Taste of Kindness
Lord, let me give from a heart of compassion, act with a desire toward kindness and extend the hand of forgiveness to those I meet today. Amen.

Be Kind to Your Soul

Your own soul is nourished when you are kind.
Proverbs 11:17, NLT

Sometimes we forget that we have all been blessed with very special attributes. We can be politicians, actors, mothers, role models for others, but there is more to us than even those things.

God places a special premium on our efforts to be kind. The feedback for your effort lies in your own soul, for it feels nourished and your heart feels light. You are walking in the way that shares the light.

How sad it is when we think that in order to succeed, or to become more in the world, we have to be aggressive in our dealings with others, perhaps even abusive. What greater success could we have than being considered both kind and compassionate in all our dealings. Your soul delights in your kindness.

A Taste of Kindness

Lord, fill my soul with joy today as I share my heart, mind and gifts of love with others according to Your grace and mercy. Let kindness rule in all I do. Amen.

Who's My Neighbor?

*"I was hungry and you gave Me something to eat,
I was thirsty and you gave Me something to drink,
I was a stranger and you invited Me in."*

Matthew 25:35-36

If you're skipping over this idea of kindness because you think you're already kind to everyone you meet, here's another perspective. Kindness is not just a nice idea, it's an action. In the community it asks you to love your neighbor as yourself.

The world is shrinking. Our neighbors are no longer simply living on our street or in our town. They live across the country, across the continent and around the world. We have endless opportunities to show kindness to others. God blesses those acts, both big and small, and fills our hearts with joy in the things we do to share His love with others.

When a stranger asks you to offer a hand of kindness, or a loved one seeks your compassion, will you be there?

A Taste of the Spirit

Lord, help me to see my neighbors as any who come across my path today. Let me offer a kind heart and a compassionate hand to their needs, to strengthen and nourish their souls and my own. Amen.

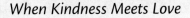

When Kindness Meets Love

*If we say we love God and don't love each other,
we are liars. The commandment that God has
given us is: "Love God and love each other!"*
1 John 4:19-21 CEV

When God's Spirit works in our hearts, it blows the wind of kindness through our bodies and moves us into action. It fills us with a desire to be more loving and to literally become a source of inspiration and renewal for others. It demands that we show Jesus to everyone. It asks us to open our hands, lift up our hearts and love like never before. We are brothers and sisters of His blood and our heritage will take us through eternity. Let's love as He loved us.

Think of all the ways you love others. How can you create even more fulfilling and loving relationships with everyone you know? Is it time for you to show your love in new ways and refresh the spirit of your relationships? God wants you to love each person in your life with His love and His joy.

A *Taste of Love*

Lord, when I think of all my Christian sisters and brothers as being part of Your family, it helps me to see each one more clearly. Help me to see each person I meet through the eyes of love today. Amen.

What Does it Mean to Be Good?

"Make a tree good and its fruit will be good,
or make a tree bad and its fruit will
be bad, for a tree is recognized by its fruit."
Matthew 12:33

"This is so good," we say, when we eat a bowl of fresh, sweet strawberries. Or we think, "Those apples are sure to make a great pie." Our mouths begin to water at the very thought of such goodness.

When we think of goodness in terms of the fruit of the Spirit, however, we might think of people who enrich our lives or who make us feel good by just being around them. We think of those who offer us encouragement or the hand of fellowship. We like to be around those people we think of as good. They make us want to be better people.

We would also like to think that most people intend to be good. We can debate that issue until the apple pie burns, but we know for certain that God is good and wants us to be good too.

A Taste of Goodness

Lord, let me honor my family by sharing the goodness of my heart and my actions with others. Help me to recognize those who need to sit in the shade of all that I've received from You. Amen.

The Good Earth

God saw all that He had made, and it was very good.
Genesis 1:31

God has big plans for the earth and for His children who inhabit it. As an example of His genuine love, imagine a Christmas morning. You've put together a beautiful doll's house for your daughter and you anticipate her delight as she sees your handiwork for the first time. After the new doll house has been thoroughly examined, you settle back to watch your child play.

A month later, you discover the window has been broken and that the house looks neglected. You start to wonder if your child did this on purpose and if you really want to fix it. Your Christmas joy diminishes.

When things started to fall apart in the Garden of Eden, God in His goodness started to make repairs. He didn't rely on our goodness, just on the incredible skill of the Carpenter.

A Taste of God's Goodness

Lord, bless the things I do today, so that I am ready with my tool box to repair any need I find and offer the hand of friendship and goodness to the people in my life. Amen.

What Good Can You Do?

*Serve wholeheartedly, as if you were serving the Lord,
not men, because you know that the Lord will
reward everyone for whatever good he does.*
Ephesians 6:7-8

What if you were walking along the street one day and you saw a sign that said, "$5,000 reward for anyone caught in the act of doing good?" Would you pay particular attention to every little deed you did that day and keep looking for the reward police to come along and give you the money? Would you try to outdo others in your acts of goodness?

Of course, it would be interesting to see how we would respond to such a sign, but then God has already posted that sign for us. He grants eternal life to all those caught in the act of believing in His Son. You can show you believe in Him by serving each other wholeheartedly. You can serve each other as if you are serving God. You have a chance every day to do good. Your reward is absolutely certain.

A Taste of Doing Good

Lord, help me to do good things for others without even thinking about it. Make it such a natural part of me that it's reward enough to have had the privilege to do it. Amen.

The Gift of Goodness

*Every good and perfect gift is from above, coming
down from the Father of the heavenly lights,
who does not change like shifting shadows.*
James 1:17

Advertising influences our choices every day. When fashions change, we're bombarded with messages telling us to get with it, be hip, be in the now. Our once fine and dandy wardrobe becomes too drab and we need new clothes. Suddenly we're behind the times just because a magazine says so.

Change is a constant thing and we can't keep it from happening. In fact, if you lived through bell bottoms in the seventies, you may agree that change in style is probably a good thing. There's a gift in change, and there's also a gift in recognizing the good in what we have right now.

The One who is the same yesterday, today and tomorrow, keeps the good in our lives a constant. The gift of His Son will never go out of fashion.

A Taste of Goodness

Lord, I may not always be up to date with the latest styles and trends. Please help me today as I put on the helmet of salvation. It may be old-fashioned, but it seems to fit me well. Amen.

I Don't Have a Thing to Wear!

Therefore, as God's chosen people, holy and dearly loved, clothe yourselves with compassion, kindness, humility, gentleness and patience.
Colossians 3:12

Some days, I look into my closet and see the sizes I want to be, the ones I used to be, the ones I am, and God forbid, the ones I hope never to be again. I select an outfit based more on what offends my pride the least than on where I'm going. This struggle always leaves me feeling that I don't have a thing to wear. But when I add the right scarf, I feel a bit better and carry on with my day.

If we could stop judging ourselves, and choose our daily wardrobe as a beloved child of God, things might be different. We can complement each other with the colors of compassion, the flowers of kindness, and the scarf of patience. Then, each time we pass a mirror, we'll see the reflection of how beautiful we really are. God has already clothed you in the gifts of His love. Wear them well!

A Taste of the Spirit
Lord, help me to dress appropriately today. I'll put on the sweater of gentleness, the blue jeans of compassion and the scarf of Your grace wherever I go. Amen.

The Fruit of Kindness

Love is patient, love is kind.
1 Corinthians 13:4

You are a kind person. You offer encouragement to those around you. You smile at complete strangers to remind them that they've been noticed and that life is good. You lend a hand whenever duty calls, and you bake a cake for the church social without batting an eye. Your kindness causes your spirit to rejoice. It causes your heart to be glad.

It is in doing those kind deeds that you get a glimpse of the heart of God, a sense of the awesome level of kindness He holds toward you and all of His creation. Breathe it in. Share it. Be kind and shine the light of God's love to those in need. You'll find them every place you go.

A Taste of Kindness

When I forget to reach out, when I am too busy to lend a hand, when I no longer have a moment to shine Your light, then be patient with me, Lord. Turn me again in the direction of Your love that I may create opportunities to be kind. Amen.

It's Time to Party

*For seven days celebrate the Feast to the LORD your
God at the place the LORD will choose. For the LORD your
God will bless you in all your harvest and in all the
work of your hands, and your joy will be complete.*

Deuteronomy 16:15

Sometimes we forget to celebrate life. We forget to
stop and give thanks for all that we've accomplished
with God's help and just celebrate His goodness.
God commanded the Israelites to take a break and
let God share in the good things they had done.
What an idea!

Do we ever think of God as the Creator of just
plain fun? Well, maybe we should. Our days are so
full, so quickly passing. We're moving at an incredible pace, doing, doing and still doing! Listen for
God's voice today and see if He isn't nudging you,
in fact, urging you to stop, to put some time aside
and discover the joy in your good work. Are you
listening? Are you having fun yet?

A Taste of Fun

Lord, help me to remember that You meant for us to
live in joy, not in a rat-race. Help me to listen for the
right moments and to live in an upbeat, joyful way for
all that You've done for me. Amen.

Giving and Lending

"Love your enemies, do good to them, and lend to them without expecting to get anything back. Then your reward will be great and you will be children of the Most High, because He is kind to the ungrateful and the wicked."

Luke 6:35

Have you ever stopped to think about how kind God really is? When we've been selfish or inconsiderate, He is still kind to us. He hears us complain, and patiently waits in kindness for us to become more of the light He meant for us to be.

According to this sixth chapter of Luke, God is even kind to the ungrateful children and the wicked ones too. Some part of me wants to politely slip by that verse in case there's any chance that I've been one of those ungrateful children. The good news is that God *gives* to us, He doesn't just *lend* to us. He's not waiting for us to pay back before He gives more. He just keeps on giving. Wouldn't it be something if we could be like that?

A Taste of Giving

Lord, help me to give more and to want less. Help me to give freely without the need or thought of getting something back. Let me give unconditionally, fully and clearly to those in need. Amen.

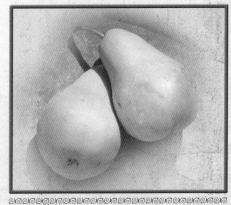

February

Guided Forever

For this God is our God for ever and ever;
He will be our guide even to the end.
Psalm 48:14

When we travel through an unfamiliar place, we are apt to engage a tour guide or at least get a book on the area to give us some direction. It's much more comfortable to know we have a sense of where we're going and what we can expect.

Psalm 48 reminds us that we have a guide who has provided a Book to help us along the way. He's prepared to show us new landscapes and He'll stay with us until the whole trip is over. Sometimes, when we use a guidebook, we're surprised to find that an incredible out-of-the-way place might not even be mentioned, while there are endless descriptions about tourist favorites. The same can be true with God's guidebook. He can lead us to incredible places we never even knew existed. We just have to have our cameras loaded and let Him know we're ready for the trip.

A Taste of Goodness

Lord, help me travel today in the direction that You would have me go, whether it's across town or out of the country, go before me and prepare the way. Amen.

Just as You Believe

*Then Jesus said to the Roman officer, "Go on home.
What you have believed has happened." And
the young servant was healed that same hour.*

Matthew 8:13 NLT

Sometimes we're pretty good at being faithful. We read the Word, we pray, and we put our belief system into practice. We might even feel we're doing a good job, at least when life is flowing along nicely and it seems most of our prayers are answered. We're generous and we give God the glory.

Then, when trials come, our strength wavers. We're not as sure God is listening or even what it means to be faithful. The centurion reached Jesus after offering his own prayers on behalf of his servant. When his own efforts didn't seem to be enough, he went straight to the Source. He just believed that Jesus could save his servant.

Today, just believe He's there to help you too.

A Taste of Belief

Lord, it is not always easy to keep believing when we can't see signs that You're near. Please help me to keep believing until I see the truth in any situation. Help me to be faithful today. Amen.

According to Your Faith

When he had gone indoors, the blind men came to Him,
and He asked them, "Do you believe that I am able
to do this?" "Yes, Lord," they replied. Then He touched
their eyes and said, "According to your faith will
it be done to you"; and their sight was restored.
Matthew 9:28-30

Most of us are not literally blind. We fumble for our glasses and get the right perspective of the world pretty quickly.

If Jesus came and stood in front of you and said He could answer a desire of your heart "according to your faith" would it happen? Would you overcome your own spiritual blindness enough to see His amazing grace for you?

Faithfulness requires us to believe that Jesus can restore our misty thoughts, our dark sides and our uncertainties. Today, may Jesus touch some area of blindness in your life and shed His light on your darkness so that you may see more clearly. May His will be done "according to your faith".

A Taste of Faith

Lord, You know that my faithfulness wavers. Help me to be faithful in the effort to overcome my own blind spots. Amen.

In Search of the Mustard Seed

"I tell you the truth, if you have faith as small as a mustard seed, you can say to this mountain, 'Move from here to there' and it will move. Nothing will be impossible for you."

Matthew 17:20-21

The fact that various mountain ranges around the world don't seem to be moving to higher ground, begs a few questions about our faith. If just a teeny, tiny seedling of faith is all that we need to launch such a marvel of nature, our seeds must not be very well rooted. If we think we have faith the size of a pumpkin seed, we're sadly mistaken.

Somehow we have to move from the ground of impossible faith to an always-possible faith. Possible faith allows us to move the mountains of doubt, despair and uncertainty that arise in our lives. Possible faith says we can hike that "fourteener," as some of those Colorado mountains are called, and keep on going. May your faith keep you moving in the direction of "all things are possible" today!

A Taste of the Possible

Lord, I know I have created more mountains than I have moved. I have fallen down more mountains than I have scaled. Help me today to have possible faith and overcome the obstacles in my path. Amen.

Childlike Faithfulness

"I tell you the truth, anyone who will not receive the kingdom of God like a little child will never enter it."
Mark 10:15

Sometimes we're a bit too adult. We lose our sense of amusement at the little things in life. We forget that we have lots of options when it comes to solving a problem. In short, we take our toys and go home when we don't think others are playing fairly.

Corporations breed tired adults who are over-worked, undervalued and seldom rewarded. Those adults then go home and feel overwhelmed by too much responsibility and too little appreciation.

Sometimes the adult in you struggles to make sense of all the theology put in front of you. Your inner-child wants to run free to believe in the simple truths of Jesus' love. Let your kingdom be ruled by your childlike faith and it will endure forever. You'll grow up in Jesus' love.

A *Taste of Childlike Faith*
Lord, I've lost my innocence. I've traded it all for knowledge and correctness, and humorless living. Help me to find You, Jesus, the way I did so long ago when I first gave You my heart. Amen.

Child of God

The Spirit Himself testifies with
our spirit that we are God's children.

Romans 8:16

When babies are born, the adoring mommies and daddies and grandmas have great fun discussing the tiny infant's beautiful features. He has Mommy's fingers and Daddy's chin, or Grandma's reddish hair. That family resemblance is the beginning of establishing the place where this child belongs.

When you were born into God's family, you started taking on some resemblance of your spiritual family. Perhaps angels said, "She has her Father's eyes, or her Creator's gift for joy, or her Savior's grace. God never makes you wonder who your Father is, for He testifies within you, establishing Himself in your spirit, to let you know that you are His. He wants very much for you to have your Father's heart and your Father's love.

A Taste of the Spirit

Lord, thank You for reminding me that I am Your child and that You have already claimed me in Your love. Help me to show You to those I meet who may need a reminder of You in their spirit today. Amen.

An "F" might be Better than All "A's"

*My message and my preaching were not with
wise and persuasive words, but with a
demonstration of the Spirit's power, so that your faith
might not rest on men's wisdom, but on God's power.*

1 Corinthians 2:4-5

Does the faith of a great preacher mean more to God than the faith of a woman with two children at home with only a little Bible training? Is there a difference in the faith of a public expression of faith and a private one? How big is your faith?

If you think you need to be an A-student to get into the program, think again. God takes a student's F from Failure to Faith and demonstrates not only His power to change lives, but also His love. Be persuaded by His love and seek opportunities today to grow in your knowledge and love for Him.

A Taste of Faith

Lord, sometimes I get so caught up in trying to better myself and my circumstances that I almost don't have time for You. I may be getting A's in life, but I'm getting F's in faith. Help me to turn that around and pay more attention to You. Amen.

Wall-flower Faith

*God did not give us a spirit of timidity, but
a spirit of power, of love and of self-discipline.*
2 Timothy 1:7

Remember those dances in high school, or maybe even junior high that you attended with your girl-friends and then one by one, they'd get invited to dance, but for some reason you hung back in the shadows and acted like it was absolutely imperative to get another cup of punch? Remember that feeling of waiting in the wings, wishing your shyness away?

Things are different now that you're older because God has invited you to the dance. No matter what music is playing, He knows you can follow Him because He's already adorned you with His love. He knows you're a powerful dancer and He doesn't want you waiting in the wings any longer. Get out there and strut your stuff for Him today. After all, He gave you great gifts for a reason.

A Taste of Self-discipline
Lord, let me rise and shine today according to Your grace and mercy. Let me take my wall-flower faith and turn it into bouquets of blessings. Amen.

Word Challenge

If you think you are being religious, but can't
control your tongue, you are fooling yourself,
and everything you do is useless.
James 1:26 CEV

My sister used to do a one-woman show where she portrayed personality styles of women through stories and poems. One story depicts a couple who are standing at Saint Peter's door trying to get in. The woman, wearing her Sunday best, rambles on about all she did at the church and how little her husband did. She insists that her goodness should get her into heaven.

After listening to her scathing comments about her husband, Saint Peter decides her husband deserves a break and sends him on alone through the pearly gates. This comment from the book of James reminds us that the biggest challenge we sometimes have is simply to keep quiet.

A Taste of Self-control

Lord, please help me to remember that every word out of my mouth either helps and encourages someone else, or hurts and diminishes someone's spirit. Challenge me to use my words wisely today. Amen.

Divine Discipline

No discipline seems pleasant at the time, but painful.
Later on, however, it produces a harvest of righteousness
and peace for those who have been trained by it.
Hebrews 12:11

Most of us don't like it when someone else tells us where we've fallen short, or what we need to do to improve our skills.

Discipline, whether it's a commitment to exercise or have a more consistent prayer life, is difficult. As children of God, we sometimes need reminders of His hopes and expectations for us and that can feel like discipline. It doesn't always feel good.

When we learn from those times, whether it's a divine thing or not, we see the value in the trial we have just passed through. We may not like the word *discipline*, especially as it applies to our level of self-control, but if we learn from it, we achieve a greater sense of peace. That could be worthwhile after all, don't you think?

A Taste of Discipline
Lord, help me now as an adult to receive discipline in a positive light, as a way to sharpen my skills in sharing my love for You. Amen.

Hoping and Praying

*Let your hope make you glad. Be patient
in time of trouble and never stop praying.*
Romans 12:12 CEV

Trouble can be a very interesting teacher. We learn a lot about ourselves when we face adversity. We discover new fears, unlimited ways to worry and renewed self-doubt.

This short verse from Romans wants us to take another view. What if we faced trouble with gladness? What if we renewed our efforts to pray with greater fervor because we believed so well in the hope that springs forth from our faith?

Your friends might look at you strangely and think you need some counseling if you smile through adversity. But could you? If you really believed in the hope that is yours as a child of God, could you? Let us patiently move through adversity and let hope radiate its light into our spirits.

A Taste of Hope
Lord, I know I'm at my worst when I'm facing a difficult situation. I try too hard to be in control and find all the right solutions. Help me, Lord, to find my hope in You today. Amen.

What Is World Peace?

*"I give you peace, the kind of peace that only
I can give. It isn't like the peace that this world
can give. So don't be worried or afraid."*

John 14:27 CEV

If you watch news programs with any regularity, it doesn't take long to recognize that we're a long way from world peace. It is interesting to think even for a moment that we could have peace according to how the world might give it.

What kind of peace does Jesus give? It's the kind that passes all understanding. If you're looking for peace with your mind, your intellect, anything but your spirit, you may not find it. Peace of the soul comes from knowing who you are, where you're headed, and that God is guiding your steps until you're safely home again. The peace the world gives may not even be a real concept. Thankfully, you have the peace that takes away fear and worry, each time you turn to Jesus.

A Taste of Peace

Lord, I get caught up in the troubles of the world and feel totally unable to control anything beyond the borders of my own home. Help me to find peace through Your Spirit each day. Amen.

Inside, Outside, Upside-down Peace

*If it is possible, as far as it depends
on you, live at peace with everyone.*
Romans 12:18

In a world where we can virtually create almost any environment we want, at least online, it's not surprising that some of us live in virtual peace. Basically, that means we've got an Advil approach to peace that makes us appear okay on the outside, while we're jumping upside-down on the inside. We mask our discontent and our concerns with smiles, denial, or anything that keeps us having to really deal with the issues.

If we really want peace, we need to find it within our own hearts and minds. We need to breathe in the spirit of contentment and hope. With peace in our hearts, we can keep connected to the God of all peace who reigns forever.

A Taste of Peace
Lord, help me sort through the chaos that floats all around me and meditate on Your goodness and Your strength. As I rest in You, may I be renewed to bring Your gift of peace to those I meet. Amen.

What Is this Thing Called Love?

"So now I am giving you a new commandment:
Love each other. Just as I have loved you,
you should love each other. Your love for one another
will prove to the world that you are My disciples."

John 13:34-35 NLT

If you're someone who celebrates Valentine's Day, you know this as the day when we remind those around us how special they are.

Love is the key to everything we do. It is the very reason Jesus came to earth. It is the embodiment of our understanding of the phrase "God is love." Wouldn't it be wonderful if we could show that kind of love to each person we meet today and every day? Spread a little love right where you are.

A Taste of Love

Lord, You have millions who look to You to lead the way to becoming more loving. Help us be Your examples of love. Amen.

Let Your Light Shine

*Feed the hungry and help those in trouble. Then
your light will shine out from the darkness, and
the darkness around you will be as bright as day.*
Isaiah 58:10 NLT

There are millions of good Samaritans living around
the world. But, sometimes we can get complacent
and start to think that there are lots of institutions,
food banks, caregivers, and missionaries taking
care of the hungry and helping those in need, so we
don't have to.

The problem is that the hungry and the ones in
trouble may well outnumber the caregivers. In each
city and village around the world there are people
desperately in need. Let us be the light and reach
out and help our neighbors. You just have to touch
one life beyond your own to make a difference.
Shine on!

A Taste of the Light

Lord, help me remember that each day there's someone
near me who is hungrier than I am, in deeper trouble
than I am, and if I just look into the warehouse of my
abundance, I can surely shine Your light on someone
else. Amen.

The World Needs More Heroes

*Let us consider how we may spur one
another on toward love and good deeds.*
Hebrews 10:24

There's nothing more motivating than seeing the
underdog win, or seeing Superman come to the rescue of some helpless victim. It's important in any
culture to create heroes, those we can emulate.

Jesus was and is a hero to many. He always
reached out with kindness, He always healed those
in great need, and He always loved the underdog.
He motivated people to want to do better and to
want to give more.

Be a hero to someone today. Just show them
what you have in Jesus and help restore them to active goodness.

A Taste of Motivation
Lord, motivate me to lead. Help me to reach out, sit
quietly, dig deeper, whatever is needed to help someone in trouble. Help me to have a hero's heart today.
Amen.

Somebody Has to Lead

*Here is a trustworthy saying: If anyone sets his heart
on being an overseer, he desires a noble task.*
1 Timothy 3:1

The call to leadership is not one to take lightly.
Whether your role is political, whether you're a
teacher or the head of your household, your leadership is important to the success of those around you.
Being in a position of authority and being a leader
are not always the same thing, however. Some come
into a power position, but still do not lead for the
benefit of their group.

Leaders look out for those in their care. A great
leader is often a great servant, and a leader shepherds his flock. How wonderful for us to have the
authority of Jesus who leads us with His love. May
we be called to the leadership of love wherever we
are. Somebody has to lead, so why don't you start?

A Taste of Leadership

Lord, I don't know how much I'm longing to lead those
around me, but I know that as a mother, a friend, a sister, a teacher, and a wife, I am often placed in that role.
Help me to lead with Your love. Amen.

Follow the Light

Your word is a lamp to my feet and a light for my path.
Psalm 119:105

We are not very comfortable with darkness. If you've ever been walking alone on a dark street, or come into the house when the day is spent and fumbled for the light switch, you know that you feel profoundly better when the light comes on.

As a child, I lived on a country road that we sometimes found ourselves walking along at night after coming from church or our neighbor's house. It was a dirt road and the cemetery was just a short way from it. I can remember praying for God to light my way home more than once. It's funny because it always seemed like the moon got ever so much brighter and I would reach our house at the top of the hill so much faster.

The good news is that God always keeps the light on for us because He wants us be sure of where we're going. He keeps us safely on the path.

A Taste of the Light

Lord, help me to walk in Your light today being sure of every step and breathing in the comfort that comes from knowing You're walking ahead of me. Amen.

Save the Planet

"I will make you a light for all nations to show people all over the world the way to be saved."
Isaiah 49:6 NCV

We love those days when we're just "on" and we can almost feel our light shining. People are receptive to us and everyone is our friend and somehow we can do no wrong.

If you're not hiding your light under a bushel, and letting it shine over all those around you, then you have the right idea. You become a light to your family, your church, your community, your state and in some way, to the world. The interesting aspect of the verse from Isaiah is that it says "I". God tells Isaiah that He will make him a light to the nations so that the world can be saved. It's a small, but important detail. Just as the moon has no light of its own, but merely reflects the light of the sun, so you have no light of your own. You merely reflect the light of the Son. He makes you shine!

A Taste of the Light
Lord, help me to reflect Your light in all that I do today. Amen.

A New Necktie

Let love and faithfulness never leave you;
bind them around your neck, write them
on the tablet of your heart. Then you will win favor
and a good name in the sight of God and man.

Proverbs 3:3-4

When you get a new scarf or a necktie, you might enjoy the fact that it is very colorful, or a sharp accent to the outfit you're wearing. A scarf or a necktie is a rather prominent piece resting just under your chin, crossing over your heart.

This proverb gives us something even more significant to wear around our necks … love and faithfulness. If you kept love and faithfulness tightly wrapped around your neck, you'd be so aware of it that nothing would get in the way of your heart.

Whether you want faithful love with your partner, or faithful love with your Savior, the more you keep close to your loved ones the better off you are. Blessed be the ties that bind.

A Taste of Love

Lord, help me to be faithful in all that I do today; in the love I share, the love I receive and the love I give to You. Amen.

Marvelous Meditation

I meditate on Your precepts and consider Your ways.
Psalm 119:15

I've been a prayer person my whole life, but in recent years, I've gained an appreciation for meditation as an addition to my prayer life. The beauty of meditation is that it allows me to focus on one major issue, joy, concern, or request at a time and often, new insights come into view. In one of my recent meditations, I asked Jesus how I could be a better light for Him. During the meditation, I found myself following Jesus up a mountain path, and I asked Him again, "How do I shine my light?"

At that point, He turned toward me, holding what looked like a virtual ball of light and He tossed it at me. I caught it somewhat incredibly, and He said, "Just *be* the light."

The insight I received from that meditation was that I didn't need to keep asking how to shine my light, I simply had to allow His light to shine through me and be the light.

A Taste of the Light
Lord, thank You for being the light for each of us and especially for me. Help me to share that light and shine for those around me today. Amen.

Mindfulness

You will keep in perfect peace him whose
mind is steadfast, because he trusts in You.
Isaiah 26:3

Have you ever thought about that old cliché about "mind over matter"? It says if you "don't mind, it doesn't matter." I know that what's on my mind matters. How I am processing things, whether I'm going off the deep end, doing my best to stay calm, or feeling all out of whack, I've discovered that things change when I change.

As soon as I let the thing I feel concerned about rest in God's care and keep my mind steadfastly on trusting Him, then peace returns to my spirit.

We're not always ready to be mindful, to be trusting, or even to be in a state of believing when things are going haywire in our lives. But if we need peace in our souls, then the lesson is to trust that Your well-being matters to God. Trust that He holds the matter in His hand and wants you to be filled with peace as things are worked out. Trust brings peace. What's on your mind really matters!

A Taste of Mindfulness

Lord, I'm not always good at handing my troubles over to You. Today, help to put my trust in You. Amen.

The Peace of God

The peace of God, which transcends all understanding, will guard your hearts and your minds in Christ Jesus.

Philippians 4:7

We are so schooled in the fine art of asking "Why?" that we sometimes forget that we don't always need to know the answer. It's actually uncomfortable for us to be in a situation where we can't intellectually reason what is going on and come out with a full understanding of the events before us. We assume that we are smart enough to figure things out.

The frustration then comes from doing all that work only to realize we still don't have the answers. We don't know why our spouse left, or why our kids made bad choices, but one thing we do know is that we can have peace in any situation. We have been offered the peace that passes understanding and protects our hearts and minds in Christ Jesus. That's an amazing offer.

A Taste of Peace

Lord, You know how much I struggle to understand things, and to solve problems so that I can come up with answers. Help me today to just rest in Your arms and let peace guard my soul. Amen.

Put on a Happy Face

May the LORD smile on you and be gracious to you.
May the LORD show you His favor and give you His peace.
Numbers 6:25-26 NLT

Each day brings a host of uncomfortable events. Maybe you have an interview with your boss at work and you just know it's not going to go well, and you have to work hard to be strong, stay positive and put on a happy face.

Whatever the situation, we spend a lot of time masking our feelings, creating faces that we hope will get us safely beyond the current crisis. The reverse of that, where we genuinely can offer our joy, our smiles, our best selves, helps us to understand this blessing from Numbers more easily. Receiving a smile from the Lord and sharing in His favor makes any day brighter. As you decide what face to wear today, check your anxieties at the door, and leave with a peaceful smile because you are in God's favor.

A Taste of Joy

Lord, help me to share the joy I have in You with those near me today. Remind me that whatever face I choose to put on, I'm reflecting my faith in Your love for me. Amen.

Discover Your Good Side

Don't just pretend that you love others. Really love them.
Hate what is wrong. Stand on the side of the good.
Romans 12:9 NLT

We are blessed to live in a world where we can speak out against injustice. We can write newspaper articles, march in parades or picket businesses. We can, but how often do we take the opportunity?

Sometimes we decide that we cannot get involved, or we have too much on our plates and we can't solve the troubles of the world because it's such an overwhelming task. That kind of thinking is certainly valid. However, sometimes opportunity will knock and ask you to stand on the side of good. Show others that you're willing to stand up for something. The old adage that "if you don't stand for something, you'll fall for anything," isn't off the mark. Stand up for love and discover your good side.

A Taste of Goodness

Lord, thank You for the freedom to express ourselves about things we believe in. Thank You for watching over the efforts of millions of activists as they strive to stand on the side of good. Help me to stand with them. Amen.

Simplifying Success

*Commit your work to the Lord,
and then your plans will succeed.*
Proverbs 16:3 NLT

We all enjoy success and aspire to achieve certain goals. How we achieve those goals can make a difference to our spirit, our health, and our family. We can become workaholics and lose sight of the other significant things around us. This proverb suggests that it can be much simpler to be successful if we just do *one* thing.

Our job is to commit our work to the Lord. The promise is that then your plans will succeed. The interesting thing is that we may lose sight of that commitment. It's more than a quick prayer as we start something new. It's deeper than that. It says those prayers must go on without ceasing, because commitment happens over time.

A *Taste of Success*
Lord, I'm making a commitment to You today to keep the work I do in Your hands. I ask that all my work be done for You and then whatever the outcome, I will have succeeded. Amen.

Out of Control!

*It is better to be patient than powerful; it is better
to have self-control than to conquer a city.*

Proverbs 16:32 NLT

I wonder what images people would choose to help them understand the significance of maintaining self-control. Proverbs says having self-control is better than conquering a city. Warriors of old, or even warriors today may not agree with that, but what does it really mean for us?

Conquering a city took a lot of soldiers and a lot of strength and muscle power, and conquering the self is a lot like this. It takes a lot of discipline, exercise and shaping up to maintain self-control.

Today we might say it is better to have self-control than to organize a march or to win an argument. If patience is power, then self-control is what conquers the city of our discontent.

A *Taste of Self-Control*

Lord, as I go about conquering my own cities today, stand beside me and remind me to move patiently among the soldiers of my peers and win by staying in total, loving control. Amen.

Shake the Dust Off

"If anyone will not welcome you or listen to your words, shake the dust off your feet when you leave that home or town."
Matthew 10:14

As a mother, a businesswoman, a wife or a friend, you have given guidance and spoken up for the things that you believe are right. When your advice or guidance was not accepted, you probably carried the weight of that conversation with you.

Sometimes we carry weights of old conversations for years, until they end up shackling us to them as their victims. We might even forget what the initial conversation was about, but we held on to the pain for so long that it has become part of our current thinking.

Matthew is speaking of carrying the gospel to others in the above verse, but it contains wisdom for everyday life as well. When you've done your best, shake the dust off your feet and move on. It will free you from taking responsibility for someone else's actions.

A Taste of Self-Control

Lord, help me to shake off the dust of those that are not mine to deal with and let the winds of Your love carry them away. Amen.

Holy Ground

*"Do not come closer," God said. "Take off your sandals,
for the place where you are standing is holy ground."*

Exodus 3:5

Have you ever stood somewhere that felt to you like holy ground? I remember a visit to Westminster Abbey in London where I was awed to be in a room where great kings are buried. I stopped to put my feet in the same place where Sir Thomas Moore was sentenced to death.

Some time later, I stood on board the Arizona outside of Honolulu. Oil still spills from it after nearly sixty years after the event that started World War II. For me it was awesome, even somewhat holy.

In a broader sense, I've learned that we are often on holy ground. We stand in our churches taking communion, we stand at altars making wedding vows, we deliver babies into the world. God places us on holy ground every time we draw near to Him, and to each other, no matter where we are.

A Taste of Goodness

Lord, help me to see the holy places that are built into my heart this day. Help me to stand in Your presence and marvel at Your works in all that I do. Amen.

March

Notable Noah

*Noah was a righteous man, blameless among
the people of his time, and he walked with God.*
Genesis 6:9

In order to understand the impact of this verse from
Genesis, I put my name in the place of Noah's. Try
it! It will give you an amazing perspective on this
passage.

Doing that exercise literally puts me in awe of
Noah and what an incredible man he must have
been. Personally, I'm grateful for Jesus who made
it possible for me to read the Scripture verse above
with my name in it. Because of His love, I can walk
with God. It's interesting to calculate how many
mistakes I've made in a few short decades, and
Noah lived to be 950 years old. I can only imagine
what havoc I could wreak in that length of time.

On the other hand, perhaps it helps us see what
good we can do in our own time, if we choose to.
Regardless of the number of days, our challenge is
to walk with God.

A Taste of Goodness
Lord, help me to become more of what You would
want me to be, and in the meantime, keep walking with
me. Amen.

The Principle of Peter

Peter began to speak: "I now realize how true it is that God does not show favoritism, but accepts men from every nation who fear Him and do what is right."
Acts 10:34-35

We live in a culture that is quick to label everything. We label kids as gifted, slow or ADD. We label our food, our clothes and our churches. We hardly miss putting a label on anything. Sometimes I wonder what would happen if we removed the labels. Would anyone really know whether the dress you wore was an Armani or Calvin Klein?

Removing labels would place a lot of things back on neutral ground. Peter's description of those who are acceptable to God reminds me that sometimes we get a little too caught up in labels. God-fearing people are found all over the world and God has labeled those people as His.

A Taste of Goodness

Lord, we know that You have people on every corner of the globe that You call Your own. Help us to remember that You don't have favorites, for You created every one of us and made us all part of Your family. Amen.

Goodness, What's Wrong?

In those days there was no king in Israel.
Everyone did what was right in his own eyes.
Judges 17:6 ESV

I would like to think that I know right from wrong and good from evil. This passage from Judges applies to us today. Many people appear to be living according to what they believe to be right in their own eyes. This would be wonderful if only what they believe in is the truth.

What happens though when people believe it's okay to steal my car from the driveway or kidnap my child? Some people live as though there are no authorities. Fortunately, we know the King who still reigns. Therefore, it is good to live according to what the King expects of you. When in doubt about whether something is right or wrong, consult with the One who reigned yesterday, who reigns today, and will reign forever.

A Taste of Goodness
Lord, help me to live according to the wishes of the King of my heart and to avoid the things that would bring You sorrow. May Your will be done today. Amen.

What Did You Say?

"I tell you that men will have to give account on the day of judgment for every careless word they have spoken."
Matthew 12:36

Do you remember every word you have spoken? I've always believed that our words are significant. Not just the words, of course, but also their intention, whether they bring healing or sorrow to someone's heart.

I don't know about you, but this passage from Matthew is downright scary. Are you ready to give account for every useless word you've ever spoken? Do you think all the good words you've spoken will cancel the bad ones?

I do know this, from today on, it will be good for you and me to be more careful of what we say and how we say it. The old phrase that you might have to eat those words might not be too far from the truth.

A Taste of Self-control

Lord, help me to remember that everything I say to uplift another person is meaningful. Let me speak only words of love today. Amen.

The Hope Within

Always be prepared to give an answer to everyone who asks you to give the reason for the hope that you have. But do this with gentleness and respect.

1 Peter 3:15

As Christians we openly declare our faith and encourage witnessing. Some of us do it with great enthusiasm while others go about it more quietly.

Christians witness by lending a hand any time we're needed or by inspiring those around us with positive spirits and generous hearts. We can do it by inviting an unexpected guest to stay for dinner. All of these deeds help us to demonstrate our faith.

Being prepared to defend your faith is not always about standing up to persecutors. More often, it's about standing up for what you believe in every day. The hope within you is the great defender Himself.

A Taste of Gentleness

Lord, since I know my hope rests in You, help me to share that hope with others today with a simple breath of kindness. Amen.

Tender Words

A gentle answer turns away wrath,
but harsh words stir up anger.

Proverbs 15:1 NLT

We've all experienced the angry words of another person, whether justified or not and we've had to choose how to respond. Would we retaliate with more anger and more harsh words? Or would we respond gently, offering the olive branch of peace?

Proverbs 15:4 says, "Gentle words bring life and health." What we say is vital to the well-being of others and to their spirit.

Today, let us remember the amazing power of words and how to offer them in kindness, gentleness, and a spirit of healing.

Saint Francis de Sales said, "Nothing is so strong as gentleness, nothing so gentle as real strength." Let your words always be for the good of another.

A Taste of Gentle Words

Lord, in every conversation, may Your Spirit prevail to bring gentleness and self-control. According to Your gifts of love and mercy, may it be so. Amen.

A Little Self-control

So think clearly and exercise self-control.
1 Peter 1:13 NLT

If you're like most people, you have days when you feel like everything in your life is simply out of control. The things that seem out of your control are not actually that important in what happens to you. More importantly is how you control yourself. You make the choices; you determine the next step and you influence the outcome.

Controlling what you say is largely about controlling what you think. What you think is controlled by what you believe about yourself and about the world around you.

How do your thoughts help you or hurt you as you respond to the world? Self-control is listed as a fruit of the Spirit and you have the ability to control your thoughts, words and actions.

A Taste of the Spirit
Lord, be in control of my thoughts and actions today. Help me to think clearly and to exercise restraint and self-control in all that I do. Amen.

Remote Control

We belong to the day, so we should control ourselves.
We should wear faith and love to protect us,
and the hope of salvation should be our helmet.
1 Thessalonians 5:8 NCV

Most of us like instant gratification. We want to push a button on the remote control of life and change the direction of things instantaneously. We want to take care of things quickly and easily with hardly any effort.

If we had such a thing as a remote-controlled life, I wonder how easily and quickly we would get ourselves into more trouble than we already are. Patience and self-control are gifts and require discipline. We need to have some idea of where we're going and what we want out of life. Generally, we can be glad that life is not always about offering instant gratification. We're blessed because discipline develops as we mature in faith. Let's be thankful we don't have push-button faith.

A Taste of Self-control

Lord, help me to learn, grow and experience life as You would have me do. I leave all that is important to me in Your hands and under Your control. Amen.

Always Be Joyful

Always be joyful. Keep on praying. No matter what happens, always be thankful, for this is God's will for you who belong to Christ Jesus.
1 Thessalonians 5: 16-18 NLT

Learning to be joyful *always* is no simple task. In fact, most of us would say that it is impossible. Why? Because it's a matter of attitude. Marcus Aurelius said, "Find joy in simplicity, self-respect, and indifference to what lies between virtue and vice. Love the human race. Follow the divine."

You might agree that one can find joy in simplicity and that you experience more joy when you are motivated by self-respect. Perhaps joy is all about loving the human race and following the Divine. Joy is a divine attribute and a divine gift.

Keep on praying, keep on following, keep on being joyful for that is your divine calling.

A Taste of Pure Joy

Lord, thank You for bringing Your Son, Jesus, into the world to create an abundance of joy in our spirits. Help us to look for His divine presence in all that we do and to share our joy with others. Amen.

So Where Do We Find Joy?

*I hope to visit you soon and to talk with you
face to face. Then our joy will be complete.*

2 John 12 NLT

One of the aspects of real joy is being with the people who mean the most to us. When Paul was traveling, he was always grateful when he returned to a city where he had many friends to share his time and thoughts with. The same is true for us.

Our joy is made complete when we welcome friends into our homes, visit family members who live far away, or even spend time with our church family. For we have greater joy when we are aligned with people who understand us and share the things that matter to our hearts.

Sharing with friends face to face is one way to experience the fulfillment of joy.

A Taste of Joy

Lord, remind me today how important and special my friends and family are. Bring us together at every opportunity to share in the fullness of Your joy and blessing. Amen.

The Joy of Jesus

*"When you obey Me, you remain in My love,
just as I obey My Father and remain in His love.
I have told you this so that you will be filled
with My joy. Yes, your joy will overflow!"*
John 15:10-11 NLT

Since joy is a gift of the Spirit, it seems reasonable to believe that God's desire for us is to live in joy. Take today and consciously embrace joy. Rise with a smile on your face, say your prayers with passion, and go about your day intending to feel every bit of joy meant for you.

You then become an ambassador of joy. Everywhere you go, you share what you have. You think of Jesus first, then others, then yourself, and by definition, you lead a life of joy, or at least a day of joy.

If you lose sight of the goal, remember that this joy comes from a place deep within you and is lit by the Spirit Himself.

Today is your day to shine!

A Taste of Joy

Father, help me remember today that You have given me a light to share with the world. Help me to shine that light in the fullness of real joy. Amen.

Taking a Joyride

*"Ask, using My name, and you will receive,
and you will have abundant joy."*

John 16:24 NLT

Wouldn't it be nice to just take a break for a day and unwind? When you've been working too hard at the office, or you have too many chores at home, you start to feel that getting out of town for a while would be a good idea. Of course, to feel like running away doesn't only happen when you need a vacation. It happens when you need joy!

Maybe you should go on a "joyride" today. Go to the park and walk around until you feel the wind in your hair. You can also pick a favorite spot by a lake and give yourself the freedom to simply relax.

Praying in your car is great because you can actually turn the radio off, and quiet things down enough to hear God and discover the joy you can only find when sharing time with Him.

A Taste of Joy

Lord, please fill me with joy today and help me focus on You and the beauty around me. Help me to see all that You have given me so that I might experience more joy. Amen.

Pride and Joy

Please keep on being faithful to the Lord.
You are my pride and joy.
Philippians 4:1 CEV

Do you know what it feels like to be someone's pride and joy? Isn't it lovely? When that person thinks of you, sees you, or embraces you, you both experience a special feeling.

Imagine what it might feel like to be God's pride and joy. What would it be like to be someone who gives Him great joy, the one He wants to talk to more often, the one He wants to hold forever?

If you can remember the feeling of being someone's pride and joy, hold on to that feeling and realize that you are indeed your Father's pride and joy. He loves you so much, He even sent His Son to redeem you.

God greatly rejoices in you.

A Taste of Joy

Lord, let me be a child again in Your presence today. Let me be Your pride and joy. Help me to honor my relationship with You in all that I do. Amen.

Cheerfully Patient

*God is the one who makes us patient and
cheerful. I pray that He will help you live at
peace with each other, as you follow Christ.*
Romans 15:5 CEV

If you are like me, you probably get impatient in
a traffic jam, lose your temper when the kids track
mud in the house, or grit your teeth when the teens
next door have one more band practice. And if you
are like me, you also probably wish you didn't get
impatient about these things.

What do you do when you find yourself mo-
mentarily losing it over the little things that come
at you during the day? How do you go back to being cheerfully patient? Can being patient ever be a
cheerful experience?

Find out. Ask God to help you when your patience is wearing thin. Ask Him to show you how to
restore your joy. He'll calm your jangled nerves.

A Taste of Patience

Lord, thank You for keeping Your banner of love over
my head, even when my head is weary and my patience
evaporates. Help me to be an example of cheerful patience in all that I do today. Amen.

Patience and Discipline

Be patient when you are being corrected!
This is how God treats His children.
Hebrews 12:7 CEV

I'm sure most of us don't think back to the discipline we received as kids with fondness and nostalgia. Some parents were too strict and others too lenient. Maybe you were lucky and yours were somewhere in between. As kids we needed discipline because it helped us to make better choices as we grew up.

God always treats you as His child. He may even discipline you when you've made some wrong decisions. How do you react? You can scowl and shake your fist, or you can be patient and understand that you are being disciplined out of genuine love.

Pray for God's guidance for the future. His genuine love and discipline will help you make better choices.

A Taste of Patience

Lord, help me be more willing to accept correction when I need it. Help me to see Your loving hand at work in my life. Amen.

Waiting Patiently

*Wait patiently for the L*ORD*. Be brave and courageous. Yes, wait patiently for the L*ORD*.*

Psalm 27:14 NLT

Waiting is difficult and we aren't very good at it. We become impatient and can't wait a second longer. So often we decide to take action, even if we aren't sure what we're supposed to be doing.

If patience is a virtue, then waiting should be on the same level. When you think about it, we're used to *instant* everything. We don't have to chop wood to build a fire and we don't have to write a letter and put it in the mail. We just have to turn on a switch, send an e-mail or go to the store.

Waiting is not one of our strong points. It can be an excellent teacher though. Next time you have to wait for something, pray. Keep praying until the waiting is over.

A Taste of Waiting

Lord, I am not very good at waiting patiently for things. Help me to see the value of waiting for results. Help me to wait patiently for Your will to be done in my life. Amen.

Patience and Perseverance

*Pray at all times and on every occasion in the power
of the Holy Spirit. Stay alert and be persistent
in your prayers for all Christians everywhere.*
Ephesians 6:18 NLT

It is when you need answers to something really important to you, that patience and perseverance come into play.

It's not easy to wait for those answers, but the good news is that you don't have to sit around and do nothing while you wait. You can wait, persevere and offer prayers. Martin Luther said, "Rest in the Lord: wait patiently for Him."

Whatever you need, be patient. Persevere in prayer and God will surely mold you into the right shape. He will answer your prayers.

A Taste of Patience

Lord, help me to persevere in prayer for the concerns on my mind and heart today. Help me to wait patiently for Your answers. Amen.

Faith, Faithful, Faithfulness

It is good to proclaim Your unfailing love in the morning, Your faithfulness in the evening, accompanied by the harp and lute and the harmony of the lyre.

Psalm 92:2-3 NLT

We talk about faith and we work at strengthening our faith and our understanding of matters of faith. We try to be among the faithful in the ways that we share our faith and live our faith each day. We exhibit faithfulness as a seasoning to our daily lives. We sprinkle it among our activities and hope it serves us well.

The psalmist suggested that we proclaim, announce and declare every morning that God loves us and that we know He is still with us as evening falls. Take a moment, listen to soothing music and meditate on God's faithfulness.

A Taste of Faithfulness

Lord, thank You that Your love never ends. Thank You that each morning and each evening I can count on You, no matter what's going on in my life. Play Your music in my heart forever. Amen.

The Grapes of Faithfulness

*By His mercies we have been kept from complete destruction.
Great is His faithfulness; His mercies begin afresh each day.*
Lamentations 3:22-23 NLT

Don't you love the thought that God is so faithful to you? Can you even grasp what it means? For one thing it means God is there for you any time you call on Him. He never sleeps. He's never busy at the neighbor's house. He's always available to you. That is faithfulness!

Couple the idea of His faithfulness with the fact that His mercies are new and fresh every single day. That means you're not waking up and relying on yesterday's quota for mercy and hoping there's enough left for today. God has a fresh quota for you every day. You can pick a new bunch of mercies like grapes from a vine because you are indeed part of the real Vine.

Live today in the abundance of God's grace and mercy!

A Taste of Faithfulness

Lord, I confess that I can't begin to understand Your kind of faithfulness. I am in awe of Your tender mercies and I'm grateful each day that I can trust in You. Amen.

Well Done!

"The master was full of praise, 'Well done, my good and faithful servant. You have been faithful in handling this small amount, so now I will give you many more responsibilities. Let's celebrate together!'"

Matthew 25:21 NLT

Nearly all of us thrive when we are praised. We try harder, are willing to work longer and take on more responsibilities. We always feel better when we know someone appreciates the work we do. "Well done!" is not a phrase that we take lightly.

As you think about that today, look for opportunities to offer praise to those around you. Salute a co-worker who has gone beyond the call of duty to help you. Reward your son with a warm smile for picking up his clothes in his bedroom. Whatever you find noteworthy in another today, be sure to offer that person a heartfelt bit of praise. Nothing is more motivating than being told, "Well done!"

A Taste of Faithfulness

Lord, help me to be faithful in offering a word of praise, or a kind comment to those around me today. Let me not hesitate to say, "Well done!" when it is richly deserved. Amen.

The Heart of Faithfulness

Your faithfulness is as enduring as the heavens.

Psalm 89:2 NLT

If faithfulness is part of the fruit of the Spirit, then the seed was planted when you took a leap of faith at some point in your life. You knew that God really had a personal message for you and you didn't want to leave His vineyard.

For any seed to grow, conditions have to be right. The gardener needs to supply the best soil, nutrients and water. He then has to be faithful to what he plants. Sometimes you're the seed, sometimes your faith is the seed. Other times, you're the gardener tending the young faith of others and helping that faith to grow.

Think about your faith-garden right now. How is it growing? Is it flourishing or is it drying up and being choked by weeds? Are you in need of help from the Master Gardener?

Your heart knows the answer.

A Taste of Faithfulness

Lord, open my heart and mind to Your tender care. Help me to grow in faith and in faithfulness toward You all the days of my life. Amen.

Having Faith in Yourself

What is faith? It is the confident assurance
that what we hope for is going to happen.
It is the evidence of things we cannot yet see.
Hebrews 11:1 NLT

You might have someone admonish you, by saying you need to have more faith in yourself. Usually they're trying to boost your confidence and your belief that you can accomplish something you've set as a goal. It's important to believe in yourself.

The source of any kind of faith is ultimately the faith we have in our Creator. It is faith that keeps us trying when we fail and keeps us praying when we're waiting for an answer.

Today, have enough faith in yourself to know that you are utterly loved by the one true God and that He indeed has great faith in you.

A Taste of Faithfulness

Lord, thank You for having faith in me. Help me to believe in the gifts You've given me and help me to use those gifts to Your glory. Amen.

Lighten Up!

Therefore, since we are surrounded by such a huge crowd of witnesses to the life of faith, let us strip off every weight that slows us down, especially the sin that so easily hinders our progress.

Hebrews 12:1 NLT

At the beginning of spring, people start jogging and try to lose some of the weight they have gained during the winter. They feel more free, less confined, and more capable of going the distance.

Your faith needs that same spring makeover. It's always there waiting to be set free in your life, to be lifted from the mire of everyday worries and habits that only serve to weigh you down.

If your faith needs a little dusting off, get started today. Take it out for a spin and see if you don't feel a whole lot lighter going around the next bend.

A Taste of Faithfulness

Lord, help me to let go of my worries and concerns and to rely more fully on the faith that I claim in You. Help me to run the race of the faithful and let nothing hinder my progress. Amen.

Peace Within

Work hard at living in peace with others.
Psalm 34:14 NLT

What can you do to live in peace today? What attitude can you adopt to help you remember your goal of maintaining peace within and peace without?

Maintaining a sense of peace requires practice. It is something you must do purposefully because it can easily be lost. One small criticism from a friend or co-worker, rejection when you expected approval, one harsh thought to yourself can disturb you and cause peace to evaporate. When anything happens to you that attempts to steal your peace, be ready with a positive way to deflect it and defend yourself. Take out your shield of faith and stand firm. It will be well worth the effort.

Hold on to your peace, share your peace, live in peace.

A Taste of Peace

Lord, help me to live in Your peace today. Help me to accomplish my goal of having peace within. Amen.

We Belong to Each Other

"So love truth and peace."
Zechariah 8:19 NLT

Mother Teresa said, "If we have no peace, it is because we have forgotten that we belong to each other."

A lot of congregations have a time for people to shake hands with each other and wish each other God's peace during the service. It's a wonderful experience that should echo in our lives as we leave the sanctuary and head out into the parking lot.

Sharing peace with others means we understand that we have a role to play in their peace. It means that what happens to them affects our lives as well. We offer them this sacred gift because we know it is the most valuable asset we have to share.

Today, pray and be at peace with yourself and with God, and then share that peace with someone else. It will do you both good.

A Taste of Peace

Lord, it isn't always easy to remember to share Your peace with others. Help me today to be an instrument of peace, according to Your will and purpose. Amen.

Right in God's Sight

*Therefore, since we have been made right in God's
sight by faith, we have peace with God because
of what Jesus Christ our Lord has done for us.*

Romans 5:1 NLT

One way to create peace in our daily lives is to remain right in God's sight. When we do that, we experience prolonged peace and joy. When we don't
do that, we experience the chaos of the world.

Remaining righteous in God's sight is a continual challenge, and without Jesus, it may not even
be possible. In fact, most of us can't remain right
for thirty seconds because while we're trying to be
right, some wicked thought comes careening over
the goal post when we aren't looking and so we run
with it. We might carry the ball, but we lose our grip
on our peace.

God's divine interception saves us again. Jesus
brings us to the winning goal of peace. Staying close
to the goal will make your day a whole lot brighter.

A Taste of Peace

Lord, it's so hard to maintain peace and stay right in
Your sight. Help me to seek Your will in all that I do and
to walk as close to You as I can today. Amen.

Signs of Peace

How wonderful it is, how pleasant,
when brothers live together in harmony!
Psalm 133:1 NLT

As a young kid, growing up in the sixties, I couldn't help but notice the peace signs that were heralded on bumper stickers and tattooed on biceps.

It was a great reminder that people are important and that war should not be taken lightly. Personally, I think it was an important crusade and one that needs to continue. We need to always strive for peace and do our best to promote peace.

All of us need to be peacekeepers. We need to share peace, make peace, and honor peace at all times. That's how we'll get to live in harmony with all of our neighbors. God wants us to be peacemakers!

Peace to you today!

A Taste of Peace

Lord, help me be a peacemaker. Let me share Your peace with everyone I meet today. Amen.

Be Kind, Please!

Be kind to each other.
Ephesians 4:32 NLT

Albert Schweitzer once said, "Constant kindness can accomplish much. As the sun makes ice melt, kindness causes misunderstanding, mistrust and hostility to evaporate."

When we see ice melting, we should remember these words. Perhaps it's time to offer more kindness to those around you and usher in its warmth. Kindness makes a difference.

Today, if you can think of anyone who needs a tender touch of kindness, something you can provide in a generous dose, then send it their way. Be the ambassador of kindness wherever you go. Kindness won't cost you a thing, but it will enrich your life enormously.

A Taste of Kindness

Lord, I do try to be kind to those around me, but help me today to be especially aware of those that might not receive enough of the milk of human kindness. Amen.

Just a Kind Word

Gentle words bring life and health.
Proverbs 15:4 NLT

Think of the kindest person you know. What is it about this person that always warms your heart and makes you glad to be in her presence? It may be some gentle way she has of doing good deeds without even seeming to notice what a great help she is to others. Or it may simply be that she always seems to know just what to say to make you smile. You always feel safe in her presence.

Being a person who offers kind words is a gift. It's a beautiful gift that seems to be scattered among a few. Of course, most of us are kind in many ways, but the kindest person you could think of is in a different category. Let's try to be kind like these wonderful people.

A Taste of Kindness

Lord, thank You for the example of my friend who is so kind. Remind me that You inspire me to share more gifts of kindness with others. Amen.

Patience and Self-control

*It is better to be patient than powerful; it is better
to have self-control than to conquer a city.*

Proverbs 16:32 NLT

Power is a key that can unlock odd behavior in people. Most situations generally allow for one person
to be in a position of power and someone else to be
subordinate. It's true of kids on the playground as
well as people in a boardroom.

What leaders in power sometimes forget though,
is where their power comes from. Regardless of
what they think, they are only in the position they
hold because God has allowed them to be there.

The message today is to remember that true
power only exists in God Himself. Others at best
only imitate Him. The measure of anyone is what
he does with the power he is given.

A Taste of Power

Lord, help me to be balanced where power is concerned. While leaning on Your power and trusting in
what You have given me, help me to patiently grow in
Your name. Amen.

Love and Fruitfulness

*"You did not choose Me. I chose you and sent you
out to produce fruit, the kind of fruit that will last.
Then My Father will give you whatever you ask for
in My name. So I command you to love each other."*
John 15:16-17 CEV

Being part of the Vine carries a responsibility. At
some point, you're expected to flower and bloom
and produce fruit. One form of that fruit is love, for
it is the kind of fruit that will last.

The various forms of love shown on television
and movie screens today seldom depicts the meaning of real love. In fact, they leave many of us uncertain as to what genuine love really is. Whatever our
human experience is with love, we always need to
go back to the Source of love when in doubt. After
all, He chose you to bear fruit. He can also teach you
the truth about what love is.

The Vinedresser knows exactly what you need
and sends you out today to share His love.

A Taste of Love

Lord, let me bear the fruit of Your love and share it with
those I meet today. Teach me how to love according to
Your will and purpose. Amen.

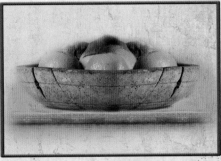

April

Being Good or Being Better!

*Remember that the Lord will reward
each one of us for the good we do.*
Ephesians 6:8 NLT

Have you ever stopped to think about the things in your life that you would like to improve on? Maybe you'd like to be a better dancer, or a better friend, or even a better cook. What do you do when you make a decision like that? Of course you take dance lessons, or cooking lessons or join the hospitality committee at church. You do all that because you'd like to go from good to better.

The same concept is true in terms of the good work you do for the Lord. Are you good at what you do? Is there anything you could do to produce more fruit, to be better at sharing what God has given you? Is it time to brush up your skills and discover what you can do even better?

Today is your first day to go from being good to being better.

A Taste of Goodness

Lord, I want to be better at sharing my heart and doing good things for the people in my life. Help me to desire to do more than I've been doing. Give me a few lessons if I need them. Amen.

Doing a Little Good

*Share every good thing you have with
anyone who teaches you what God has said.*

Galatians 6:6 CEV

Each of us is blessed with abilities. We can use those
abilities to do good any time we choose. Sometimes
we don't work for the good of others simply because we assume that our contribution as just one
person will be too small any way. How much good
can one person do, we might wonder?

If you choose today to go out and do a little
good, what will happen? The truth is that you don't
know. What looks like one person doing a small
thing, may turn out to be more important than you
realize.

Think about David and Goliath. It's not always
about numbers, or about being the biggest or the
strongest. It's not always even logical. Sometimes,
it's just about a few well-placed stones.

A Taste of Doing Good
Lord, You have blessed me with some great gifts that I
can share to bring good into Your kingdom. Help me to
reach out and have an impact today. Amen.

Joy Is an Action Word

"Ask and you will receive, and your joy will be complete."
John 16:24

Edward Everett Hale once said:

> *I am only one, but still I am one.*
> *I cannot do everything, but still I can do something;*
> *And because I cannot do everything*
> *I will not refuse to do the something that I can do.*

If we want to experience true joy, the spirit of joy that God meant for us to have, we have to do something. We have to be willing to step outside ourselves and reach out to others. It's true we can't do everything, but we can pick one cause, one charity, one family, one friend, one something that will become the object of our help and our kindness.

What one thing are you willing to do? Ask God to guide you to where He most wants you to share your joy.

A Taste of Joy
Helping others does make me feel good, Lord. Deepen my desire to reach out in a new direction to offer Your joy to others. Amen.

Great Kindness

I now place you in God's care. Remember
the message about His great kindness!
Acts 20:32 CEV

Paul was a man of action. From the day the Lord gave him a new vision on the road to Damascus, until the day he wrote this letter before going to jail for preaching the Good News, Paul stayed on the job. His journey from blindness to sight is our journey too. We are in God's care, the recipients of His kindness. We may also be working through some blindness ourselves in one area of our lives or another.

Are your eyes open to the fact that you are a recipient of God's kindness? Have you noticed His hand at work in your life, sustaining you and encouraging you? Take it upon yourself today to be more conscious of all that God is doing in your life. Open your eyes and celebrate His kindness to you.

A Taste of Kindness

Lord, You are ever present in my life and I thank You and praise You for loving me so much. Help me to receive Your great kindness and share it with those who need more of You. Amen.

Ambassadors Forever

We are Christ's ambassadors,
and God is using us to speak to you.
2 Corinthians 5:20 NLT

We usually think of ambassadors as emissaries of goodwill who hope to bring people together and help them understand one another better. They are masters of communication and understand how people think, feel and react to life. As someone with the gift of goodness, you are indeed an ambassador for Christ.

Being an ambassador means that you can help others to know God. You help bridge the gap between what they understand about God and what the truth is. You are the messenger who brings them hope.

When you signed up to be a Christian, you took this role for life. May God bless you with opportunities to shine for Him.

A Taste of Goodwill

Lord, I don't always remember that I have a full-time job with You. I'm never unemployed. You always have work for me to do and I thank You. Amen.

Being Salt

"You are the salt of the earth.
But what good is salt if it has lost its flavor?"
Matthew 5:13 NLT

We tend to group things together according to their value. We might put small things that happen to us in one category and big things in another, yet each has an impact. Sometimes the small things together can become great and change your life.

Salt is a good example. Salt consists of small white particles that enhance the flavors of food. Those small particles have a lot of power! What happens when salt loses its saltiness? What happens when you lose your "saltiness" for God?

Since you are the salt of the earth, you make a difference. You are important to the well-being of those around you. Your saltiness helps flavor their faith and their actions. What can you do to enhance their lives a little more today?

A Taste of Salt
Lord, help me be like salt. Help me add flavor, richness and desire in the hearts of those around me to know You better. Let me shake their lives with Your Spirit. Amen.

Don't Bug Me!

We give great honor to those who endure under suffering.
Job is an example of a man who endured patiently.

James 5:11 NLT

Most of us don't want to have the patience of Job.
We don't want to suffer anywhere near the number
of things he endured, yet we're overwhelmed by
little things.

Most of your troubles are small, but they have
the same power as a mosquito that flies around
your head when you're trying to sleep. It's a small
thing, but you know that any minute it might swoop
down in search of your blood. Before long you can't
sleep because you've got to conquer the source of
your trouble.

Patience is hard to have when every problem
feels more like a hovering mosquito. Stop letting
the little things become big things. Thank God for
the things you *don't* have to endure. Then the mosquito's humming will stop.

A Taste of Patience

Lord, I really don't like having all the little things in my
life become so annoying. I'm sorry that I've given them
more power than they deserve. Help me to patiently
rest in You. Amen.

The Love of God

Understand, therefore, that the LORD your God is indeed God. He is the faithful God who keeps His covenant for a thousand generations and constantly loves those who love Him and obey His commands.

Deuteronomy 7:9 NLT

You are loved by the God of the universe, the Creator of all things, the One who is indeed God. His love remains with you constantly. His love asks only one thing ... obedience.

How do obedience to God and understanding relate to one another? Oswald Chambers said, "The tiniest fragment of obedience, and heaven opens up and the most profound truths of God are yours straight away. God will never reveal more truth about Himself till you obey what you already know."

Getting to understand the will of God in your life and growing in His truth have everything to do with your desire to be obedient. Being obedient has everything to do with your desire to love Him.

A Taste of Love

Dear Lord, help me to be faithful to Your love by being obedient to Your desire for my life. Help me to walk closer to You each day. Amen.

There's No Spiritual Fruit called Anger

*Those who control their anger have great understanding;
those with a hasty temper will make mistakes.*

Proverbs 14:29 NLT

Self-control comes in many forms. We need self-control when it comes to spending our money or indulging our sweet tooth. We need it in relationships and it is especially necessary when we feel anger taking root within us.

What happens when we give in to anger? Often, it just escalates the problem, causes needless distance in relationships, and raises our blood pressure. None of these are helpful to the situation at hand.

If controlling anger increases understanding, it is definitely worth a try. Next time you find yourself seething under the skin, stop, think, pray, give it to God and then create a response that is worthy of the issue. Hasty decisions made in anger are often regretted.

A *Taste* of Self-control

Lord, help me to remember that reacting in a negative way never helps solve the problem. Help me to listen to Your voice when I am faced with feelings of anger. Amen.

When the Winds of Anger Blow

*A fool gives full vent to anger, but
a wise person quietly holds it back.*

Proverbs 29:11 NLT

When are you most likely to experience a power shortage? When you choose to vent your anger and let the storms in your mind rage against another human being.

As soon as you begin to vent your anger, you give away your power. The other person now controls not only the situation but you as well. How? The other person uses wisdom and self-control. Anger extinguishes your lamp of wisdom. You become the fool.

When you feel the winds of anger blowing around you, don't give in. In fact, give over every feeling you have to God and let Him help you stay in control. You'll come out the winner in the long run. Anger has never been a good guide. Don't blow it! It's time to stay calm.

A *Taste of Self-control*

Lord, as You walk with me today, help me to remain in Your care and keeping. Keep me in gentle breezes and calm spirits. Amen.

Stolen Peace

Don't worry about anything; instead, pray about everything.
Tell God what you need, and thank Him for all He has done.
If you do this, you will experience God's peace, which is far
more wonderful than the human mind can understand.

Philippians 4:6-7 NLT

How much does worry cost? Does it cost you a good night's sleep? Does it take away from the joy you should be having at your daughter's birthday party because your mind is somewhere else? Does it steal your vacation right out from under your feet? What does it cost you?

Worry is very expensive. It often causes poor health in body and mind. How can you afford one more day of it? Stop worrying today. Pray about everything and put your anxieties in God's hand. If you place your troubles at the foot of the cross, you can experience peace from God, which is a true gift of the Spirit.

A Taste of Peace

Lord, I surrender my worries to You and place them at the cross. I know You've already paid my debt and You're willing to carry my burdens. Thank You for loving me so much. Amen.

To Be or Not to Be!

"I am leaving you with a gift – peace of mind and heart. And the peace I give isn't like the peace the world gives. So don't be troubled or afraid."
John 14:27 NLT

Perhaps you've been through times in your life when you prayed hard for peace of mind. You told God you'd do anything for that peace. However, every time you tried to work, shop or talk to a friend, your anxiety returned and you had no peace.

Why? "Know God, know peace" the saying goes. Yet you do know God and you're not at peace. Perhaps it's a matter of degree. Do you know God like you know a distant cousin or the guy who sits in the back row at church Sunday after Sunday? Or do you know God like you know your dearest friend?

Whether you are anxious or not depends on your friendship with God. Perhaps today is a good day to renew your friendship and receive His gift of peace of mind.

A Taste of Peace
Lord, I want to live in Your peace and dedicate today to You. Help me to accept Your gift of a peaceful mind and heart. Amen.

Renewing Your Mind

*Let the Spirit change your way of thinking and make
you into a new person. You were created to be like
God, and so you must please Him and be truly holy.*
Ephesians 4:23-24 CEV

Learning to be faithful is a process and it means
you have to understand what it will take for you
to become what God intends. As a Christian, you
are continually learning and being challenged to
change your way of thinking. You are striving to
become more holy.

It is fairly safe to say that you may never learn
all the rules. Oh, you'll have the basic foundation
under your feet, but even the simplest concepts will
suddenly stretch you into a new shape when the
Spirit leads. You'll be forced to rethink and recon-
sider the thoughts of the past. Even learning to love
others will take on a new dimension.

It's time to renew your mind with the help of the
Spirit of God.

A Taste of Faithfulness
Lord, every time I think I understand what it means to
love my neighbor, I discover a new neighbor I'm not so
sure I like, much less love. Create in me the desire to be
a more loving person in faithful service to You. Amen.

The Golden Rule

"Treat others just as you want to be treated."
Luke 6:31 CEV

By now, you've probably learned that most people are apt to treat you the same way you treat them. There are some who persist in their efforts to keep people at a distance by being snippy and staying aloof, but that's not the general rule. It is all about attitude.

You may say attitude is not a fruit of the Spirit and you'd be right, except that attitude is an overarching aspect of all the gifts you receive. If you treat others with respect and believe in their goodness, then that attitude is helping you with the gift of goodness.

If you have a strong, positive attitude, your mind and heart will more quickly align with the gifts of the Spirit and you'll benefit more fully from them. When you treat others with love, they respond with love.

A Taste of Attitude
Lord, help me to have a more positive attitude about people and about life and about the work I do. Create a deep desire within me to treat everyone well. Amen.

Peacekeepers

"God blesses those who work for peace, for they will be called the children of God."

Matthew 5:9 NLT

Perhaps you have never been actively involved in a peace campaign. You may have donated some money to organizations promoting world peace or you may pray for peace every day. Perhaps your contribution seems insignificant but the fact that you desire peace proves that you are a child of God

Beyond the task of helping to keep peace in the world, you can be a peacekeeper in your own home and at work. There's always a need for those calm souls with an ability to reason to guide the course toward peace.

Blessed are you if you're a peacemaker. Make it your business wherever you are today to create peace. Help bring discord to its knees.

A Taste of Peace

Lord, I may not be able to make a difference in an assembly of peace marchers today, but I can make a difference in my own home and my own neighborhood. Bless my efforts to share Your peace today. Amen.

Doing Good Deeds

For our people should not have unproductive lives.
They must learn to do good by
helping others who have urgent needs.

Titus 3:14 NLT

Sometimes we hesitate to be a "do-gooder." We don't want to be labeled for the very thing that we are instructed to become. Doing good is not something we should ever become weary of and in fact, there is no end to the good we can do if we're willing.

If we're young, we think we can't do good because we're just kids. If we're married with young children, we think we don't have time to do good. If we're in the process of working our way up the ladder, we think we're too busy to do good. When we retire, we think we're too old to do good.

When do we do good then? Those in urgent need do not necessarily exist in third world countries, some exist in your own neighborhood. Reach out. Do something good for someone else today. It's time.

A Taste of Goodness

Lord, remind me of all the ways that others have done good things for me and help me to look for ways to do good to others every chance I get. Amen.

An Attitude of Joy

Let every created thing give praise to the LORD,
for He issued His command, and they came into being.
He established them forever and forever.
Psalm 148:5-6 NLT

Praising the Lord always creates an attitude of joy. You cannot praise Him with all your heart, mind and soul and not be instantly lifted into the heavenly realms of grace and joy. He transports your spirit and brings it closer to Him with every echo of praise that falls from your lips.

An attitude of praise is very much like an attitude of prayer. You need to surrender to it, release the day's concerns, the circumstances that are out of your control and the weariness of your heart. Reach up to Him and bask in the glory of His goodness. Remind Him once again how much you love Him for all He has done for you. Let your praise produce an attitude of joy.

Sing your hosannas!

A Taste of Joy

Lord, I don't always remember to thank You for the wonderful things You have done for me, especially the gift of Your Son, Jesus. I praise You, Lord, with all my heart. Amen.

It's a Matter of Where You Look

Search for the LORD and for His strength, and keep on searching. Think of the wonderful things He has done.
Psalm 105:4-5 NLT

A good part of your faithfulness is about your approach. It's about how you think and where you look for strength. It's about the trust you place in God.

Edward Everett Hale reminds us, "To look up and not down, to look forward and not back, to look out and not in, and to lend a hand." When faith looks up, it is inspired to search for God. When faith looks forward, it is trusting in His promises. When faith looks outward, it sees God's love everywhere and when faith lends a hand, it moves to take care of God's own.

As you search for renewed strength and continued faithfulness, remember to look up and think of the wonderful things God has done for you.

A Taste of Faithfulness

Lord, remind me always that You are with me in all that I do. Help me to look for opportunities to strengthen my faith in You by serving those around me. Amen.

Being the Gatekeeper

I would rather be a gatekeeper in the house of my God than live the good life in the homes of the wicked. For the LORD God is our light and protector. He gives us grace and glory.

Psalm 84:10-11 NLT

You could see the gatekeeper as the person who decides who enters or leaves, or as a janitor who keeps things in order. But what is important about the gatekeeper is his faithfulness. Your faith determines where you stand on any given day, about any important issue, and with any group of associates. You decide what it means to have "the good life."

For a person of faith, "the good life" is lived in service to God. That service is about sharing in His presence and His goodness, His light and His protection every day. You're the gatekeeper and it's important for you to determine exactly where you want to stand.

A Taste of Faithfulness

Lord, it's not always easy to stand tall for You. It's hard because there are so many options and the "good life" as the world defines it is pretty tempting. Help me to be more faithful to You and to be a better gatekeeper. Amen.

Have No Fear

*All who listen to me will live in peace
and safety, unafraid of harm.*
Proverbs 1:33 NLT

It's not easy to have peace within your soul these days. Five minutes of watching CNN or reading the paper makes you feel anxious. If you're not worrying about the environment and concerns about the welfare of people all over the world, then you're concerned about terrorists who have no regard for human life.

You may not have control over the forces of nature or over people who continually try to wrap you in a blanket of fear, but you do have control over how you think about those things. You can give your fears to God and pray for His protection. You can ask Him each day to keep you safe and help you maintain peace in your heart. You truly can have a sense of peace and well-being. It's yours for the asking.

A Taste of Peace
It is so hard, Father, to understand all the things that go on in the world today. Please protect me and those I love and keep us safe from harm. Amen.

Finding the Good Fruit

A healthy tree produces good fruit, and an unhealthy tree produces bad fruit ... The way to identify a tree or a person is by the kind of fruit that is produced.
Matthew 7:17, 20 NLT

How do you tell the difference between good and bad people? How do you know which ones are producing great fruit and which ones aren't? It isn't always easy. In our culture, we often assume that beautiful people would just naturally be good, but beauty and goodness do not always go hand in hand. Maybe our definition of beauty is wrong. We need to see that a good person is always beautiful because their goodness comes from God.

Whatever your definition of beauty is, remember that what distinguishes good people from bad is their internal goodness. The way you tell whether you're following God is to see what kind of fruit you have produced. It has nothing to do with your wardrobe or your wallet, but with your heart.

A Taste of Goodness
Lord, let me be a sweet and wholesome fruit of Your vine. Help me to share the goodness of Your love and joy with anyone who will listen. Amen.

For Your Own Good

Nobody should seek his own good, but the good of others.
1 Corinthians 10:24

Have you ever noticed what happens to you when you start to feel slightly depressed? Before you know it you're curled up in a little ball. Everything is suddenly about you and what is or isn't happening to you. For your own good, in such times, let go of thinking about yourself and rather think about others.

If you step out of your world and reach out to help someone else, you might discover that things look a lot better than they did before.

You need to learn to focus on the well-being of others and not on yourself. It's a sure cure for what ails you. It may not take away the things that made you hide out and curl up in a blanket, but it will make a difference in how you see everything around you.

A Taste of Goodness
Lord, help me remember that I'm not the only one with problems. Help me do what I can for others regardless of my own situation. Amen.

Who's Within You?

*Those who are dominated by the sinful nature think
about sinful things, but those who are controlled by the
Holy Spirit think about things that please the Spirit.*

Romans 8:5 NLT

What we carry in our minds and hearts often comes
out in what we say. We think about them as concerns, ideas or dreams that live deep within us. As
Christians though, we can also look at who's within
us.

When we make up our minds to please the Holy
Spirit, then we have surrendered that day to the
Lord Himself. When we wander in confusion, not
quite certain about ourselves or the things going on
around us, then we have given over our very center
to the world. As you approach a new day, be sure to
call upon Jesus Christ to be at the center of your
very being. When you do that, the Holy Spirit will
guide you and your thoughts into all things that
please Him.

A Taste of Self-control

Lord, some days I get caught up in all the things I have
to accomplish and the work I have to do and I lose sight
of You. Be near me today and be the center of my universe. Amen.

A Cheerful Heart

A cheerful look brings joy to the heart,
and good news gives health to the bones.
Proverbs 15:30

Why is it that some of the people you know seem to walk around with a perpetual frown on their faces? They aren't in a particularly bad mood it seems, they're just not willing to go all the way to a smile. What a difference it is when you run into a friend who always has a big smile for you, embraces you with a hug and lets you know what a joy it is just to be around you.

That kind of person not only brings a cheerful look, they bring joy too. They make life feel good. Whatever you're going to do today, take a look in the mirror before you walk out the door. You may need to adjust the most important part of your wardrobe ... your smile. See if it's there and if it's ready to meet the world and then share it with everyone you see.

A Taste of Joy

Lord, I know what a big difference it makes to me when I spend time with the people who greet me with joy. Help me do the same for those I meet today. Amen.

The Oil of Joy

You love what is right and hate what is wrong.
Therefore God, your God, has anointed you, pouring
out the oil of joy on you more than on anyone else.

Hebrews 1:9 NLT

Did you wake up bathed in the oil of joy this morning? What a wonderful image that is! When we belong to Christ, we're already washed, cleaned and pressed into His service. We're anointed with His Spirit and able to do more than we ever knew was possible.

As you think of everything you hope to accomplish today, believe that all things are possible and that you are prepared, protected, and ready to deliver on the promises of God's love for you. The beauty of oils is that they are quickly absorbed by your skin, and gently work their way through your system. Imagine that you've been liberally sprinkled with the oil of joy today and go out and share some of your blessing.

A Taste of Joy

Lord, thank You for filling me with Your loving Spirit. Help me to share the joy and the blessing You've given me today. Amen.

Soften Your Heart

Today you must listen to His voice. Don't harden your hearts against Him as Israel did when they rebelled.

Hebrews 3:15 NLT

Do you find that some days you hear God's voice easily, but other days you might as well be wearing earphones, have the TV blaring and the kids yelling because nothing gets through to you? The Bible often reminds us to keep our hearts soft.

In our culture, we sometimes think of soft-hearted people as weak and powerless. We assume that one has to detach from emotion to be effective in life. Obviously, those soft-hearted people just don't understand how hard the world is! And yet, God seems to tell us to keep soft hearts, especially toward Him. That's how we can hear His voice.

Open your heart to Him today and you'll hear Him as He talks with you throughout the day.

A Taste of Soft-heartedness
Lord, I don't even realize that I have shut You out until after a while I find myself wondering where You are. Then I discover, I'm the one who closed the door. Help me keep the door of my heart open to You. Amen.

Get a Grip

So take a new grip with your tired hands and stand firm on your shaky legs. Mark out a straight path for your feet. Then those who follow you, though they are weak and lame, will not stumble and fall but will become strong.

Hebrews 12:12-13 NLT

Have you ever been to the circus and seen the performers build a human tower? One man stands while another climbs on his shoulders. Then another climbs on his shoulders again. Have you ever wondered how the man at the bottom doesn't just buckle under the weight?

If you are standing tall in the Lord, then you are the guy at the bottom of the tower because all around you are people standing on your shoulders. They are weaker than you and are in need of support from someone who is strong and stable. When God holds you in His hand, you're able to hold some of His newcomers as well. His goal is to touch each one so that none will be lost. He's counting on you to remain in His grip.

A Taste of Support

Lord, keep me in Your care and help me to strengthen the way for others to know You. Help me to stand firm in You. Amen.

Living by the Spirit

Since we live by the Spirit, let us keep in step with the Spirit.
Galatians 5:25

What does it mean to live by the Spirit? How do we keep in step with the Spirit?

If you live by a certain work ethic, you demonstrate it by everything you do. You learn everything you can about your business, and you stay up to date on the latest information about it. You talk to others about it and probably even think about it when you're not working. You sometimes live, breathe and sleep your work.

If you live by the Spirit then you do the same thing. You faithfully read the Word so you can keep up with what God has to say, you pray and listen and wait for God's direction in your life. As one with a passion, you talk about it with those around you and think about it every chance you get. You live by the Spirit in all that you do.

A Taste of the Spirit

Lord, as I try to fall into step with You today, lead me in the direction You would have me go and help me to be mindful of You in all that I do. Amen.

Just Be Patient!

Be completely humble and gentle; be patient,
bearing with one another in love.
Ephesians 4:2

Your mother was probably the first person who admonished you to be patient. You were waiting for Christmas or your birthday or for Dad to come home and she would smile and say, "Just be patient." You could hardly bear it, but you tried.

Now that you're grown, you might hear this from your spouse or your boss at work or even your friends, but waiting for something, waiting for anything is just as hard now as ever before. Just be patient!

Part of that skill is learning to be patient with yourself as well. The more you recognize that you often have to be patient with others, the more you see why the same rules have to apply to you. Be patient with yourself and see how it helps you.

A Taste of Patience

Lord, You know I'm not very good at being patient with others, much less with myself. Help me to be more of what You would have me be. Amen.

Add a Little Goodness

*For this very reason, make every effort to add to your
faith goodness; and to goodness, knowledge; and to
knowledge, self-control; and to self-control, perseverance;
and to perseverance, godliness; and to godliness,
brotherly kindness; and to brotherly kindness, love.*

2 Peter 1:5-7

If you were creating a recipe for right living, smart thinking and faithful following, the verse above would do nicely. It reads like a list of ingredients. Add a little knowledge, a pinch of godliness and a cup and a half of goodness and you'll be on the way to becoming the master chef of love. Well, maybe.

Adding goodness and self-control to your life always means you'll enjoy a little more of the good stuff life has to offer. After all, the more you give, share and offer to others in the right spirit, the more you will receive. Brotherly and sisterly kindness and love will always reward you. What will you add today?

A Taste of Goodness
Lord, help me to do whatever I do in goodness and love.
Amen.

May

God's Greatness

The LORD, your Redeemer and Creator, says: "I am the LORD, who made all things. I alone stretched out the heavens. By Myself I made the earth and everything in it."

Isaiah 44:24 NLT

Have you ever stopped to meditate on how great God is? Do you sit in awe of the fact that He is your Redeemer and Creator? He alone brought you into being and set your feet upon the earth. He alone is in control of the entire universe.

When you give God control of everything in your life, your priorities fall into place. You remind yourself that nothing exists because of you, but everything exists because of Him. Then you can give up your own need to be in control and you can even stop asking "why?" You can just let the divine greatness of God be the master of all things. Let God be God and let Him be even greater in your life.

A Taste of God's Greatness

Lord, I always thought You needed my help in getting things done. Remind me, Lord, that You are always in control because You're great enough to handle everything. Amen.

Comfort and Joy

When anxiety was great within me,
Your consolation brought joy to my soul.

Psalm 94:19

In these days there's a worldwide sense of depression and we miss God's presence in daily things because we're caught up with the news of the day that blasts away at the core of human dignity and values. We're lost and blown about in the debris of this massive consciousness.

We're *in* the world, but we don't have to be *of* the world. We can rise above it and cling to the Savior for comfort and relief. We can reach for His life preserver of faith to get us through the storms ahead. When we do, the Rock of our salvation will give us comfort and joy.

A Taste of Joy

Lord, help me to come closer to You whenever life makes me feel anxious and overwhelmed. Let me draw strength, peace and joy from Your hand. Amen.

Happy Circumstances!

Good planning and hard work lead to prosperity.
Proverbs 21:5 NLT

Most of us have a tendency to blame our circumstances when things don't go our way. We say we didn't have enough time, money, energy or support from friends. Often these factors do play a role, but are they really the reason behind the lack of success?

Part of our faithfulness to God is about not making excuses when things don't go just right. He's always available to help us create happy circumstances that will benefit our hearts and minds. We need to be faithful in the asking and in the planning.

Don't like what you see? The Creator is ready to help you make new circumstances today!

A Taste of Faithfulness

Lord, please be with me today and show me the places where I'm relying a little too much on other people's whims. Let me work with You to create the best circumstances for my life. Amen.

Sharing Peace

The Father is a merciful God, who always gives us comfort. He comforts us when we are in trouble, so that we can share that same comfort with others in trouble.
2 Corinthians 1:3-4 CEV

You may have shared peace at church this week, but as a believer, it's your job to share peace out in the world as well. God has given you His comfort. You've experienced what it feels like to bask in His presence and be renewed and strengthened by His love. That comfort fills you with an exquisite peace that others can see and feel when they are around you. You may be the only source of peace available today to those around you.

Make it a priority to share peace with those you meet everywhere you go. Offer them comfort, the hand of fellowship, and a heart to listen to their needs. After all, you're an ambassador for peace and there's a lot of peacekeeping work for you to do.

A Taste of Peace
Lord, help me to share Your peace today. For those in distress, let me offer the comfort that only You can bring. Amen.

The Commandment to Love

Jesus said, "'Love the Lord your God with all your passion and prayer and intelligence.'" This is the most important [of God's commands], the first on any list.
Matthew 22:37-38 THE MESSAGE

What can you do to honor this commandment in your life today? How can you show your love to God?

Honor God with your passion. Look at the things that make your heart sing, give you new energy and bring your spirit to life. That's the feeling that demonstrates your love for God.

Honor God with your prayers. Take everything to Him. Put your sorrows and concerns at His feet. Give Him your joys, excitement and hopes.

Honor God with your intelligence. Surrender your goals, ambitions and dreams to Him and trust Him to return to you those things that are truly yours.

Follow the commandment to love God and see what a difference it makes for you.

A Taste of Love
Dear God, I surrender my passion, my heart, my mind and my spirit to Your care and keeping. Amen.

Love One Another

*"But there is a second [command of God] to set
alongside it: 'Love others as well as you love yourself.'"*
Matthew 22:39 THE MESSAGE

Have you ever met someone who seems totally
caught up with themselves? The truth is that those
people are often struggling to show love to you because they've lost the ability to love themselves.

If the command is to "love others as ourselves"
some of us are in jeopardy. We have not been very
good at loving ourselves. In fact, we're not even really sure what it means.

If you've forgotten how to love yourself, consider
creating some ways that might renew your understanding. Give yourself a gift of honoring *you*. Take
note of each time you do something or say something or understand something about yourself that
makes your gift of joy more evident. The more you
learn to love yourself, the more you'll understand
how important it is to share that love with others.

A Taste of Love

Lord, help me to understand what it means to have
genuine self-love so that I can love others. Amen.

Compassion Brings Peace

*All of you should be of one mind, full of
sympathy toward each other, loving one another
with tender hearts and humble minds.*

1 Peter 3:8 NLT

Compassion is not about emotion, but about being willing to help people when a need arises. It's about your connection to others and your tender heart. When your heart is willing to act, your head and your hands will follow.

You can hardly read the daily paper of any city in the country without feeling compassion for people. Your compassion is called upon to help those who have just suffered great loss after a hurricane, or to volunteer your time to help build houses. When you respond in a way that does your heart good, an interesting thing happens: You're given an instant gift – peace.

Compassion is the sister of peace.

A Taste of Compassion

Dear Lord, help me to reach out with a genuine sympathy to those in need. Remind me that everything I have comes to me from Your goodness and Your grace. Amen.

Confidence in Your Faith

You were saved by faith in God, who treats us much better than we deserve. This is God's gift to you, and not anything you have done on your own.

Ephesians 2:8 CEV

Do you believe that you are saved by the grace of God and that He is ready to treat you far better than you deserve? If your answer is not a resounding yes, it's not surprising. Many people are believers and yet they do not have confidence in their faith.

Martin Luther said, "Faith is a living, daring confidence in God's grace, so sure and certain that a person would stake his life on it a thousand times." Would you stake your life on your faith?

Connect with God so richly and fully today that you don't rest without knowing that you are loved and saved by your faith in Him. If you have any doubt at all about where you stand, then talk to God and become confident of His gift to you.

A Taste of Faithfulness

Lord, help me to be sure of my salvation. Help me to live in such a way that I celebrate the joy of all that You have done for me each day. Amen.

At Peace with Yourself

I have learned, in whatsoever state I am,
therewith to be content.
Philippians 4:11 KJV

The gift of contentment, regardless of your circumstances is one you might not always have. Open your gift any time and use it as often as you'd like. It's up to you. You can be as content as you choose to be. You can be at peace in a moment's notice.

Restless hearts are not content. They search everywhere for peace to calm their stretched nerves.

You don't need to have a restless heart. You can learn to be content in whatever circumstances. You can learn to be at peace with yourself because your Father in Heaven wants you to be at peace. He has given you the gift of His peace through the Holy Spirit.

A Taste of Peace

Lord, it is not easy for me to find peace in the world, in my home and in my heart. I want to, but I'm not good at surrendering the things that make me restless. Help me today to rest in You. Amen.

On Your Way Rejoicing

This is the day the Lord has made.
We will rejoice and be glad in it.
Psalm 118:24 NLT

God made this day just for you. You can share it with your family or your friends, your co-workers or simply enjoy it by yourself. Whatever you are doing today, remind yourself that God made this day for you.

When you put on a happy face and dance a little, the world suddenly seems a bit brighter and a lot friendlier. It becomes a place where you can literally see the grace of God everywhere you go. It becomes the beautiful world God meant it to be.

Test it yourself. Go outside and give a great big smile and a friendly hello to the first three strangers you meet and see if it doesn't make you feel like rejoicing. This is the day the Lord has made, and He made it just for you. That is something to sing a little praise song about. Tap those feet! Come on!

A Taste of Goodness

Lord, remind me of Your goodness in all I do today. You have given me all that I have and all that I need and I praise You with all my heart. In Jesus name, Amen.

You're so Brave!

Be on guard. Stand true to what you believe. Be courageous. Be strong. And everything you do must be done with love.
1 Corinthians 16:13-14 NLT

What was the most recent thing you did that took real courage? Perhaps you had to speak in front of a group of people and you're not very confident about speaking in public. Or maybe you stood up for a friend that made you unpopular as a result.

You may find it takes courage to share your faith. You might wonder if this is the right person, or the right place, or the right time to witness. You might think you're around people who probably don't want to hear what you have to say.

But you're brave, you just carry on standing up for friends, sharing what you believe, being strong in the Lord. You're an example of what it really means to do everything in love. Keep on doing what you do best because it's exactly what God wants you to do.

A Taste of Faithfulness
Dear Lord, help me to have the courage to share what's in my heart, especially when my heart wants to share more about You. Amen.

No Fear!

"Don't be troubled or afraid."
John 14:27 NLT

Every generation from before Jesus' time to our present time, has experienced fear of some kind. It may have been fear of disease, war, hurricanes, or anything else. Today we fear a wide variety of things. What can you do? You're told in John 14 not to be troubled or afraid. Can your faith help you overcome your fear?

Martin Luther King Jr. said, "Courage is an inner resolution to go forward in spite of obstacles and frightening situations; cowardice is a submissive surrender to circumstances."

If reading the newspaper causes distress, stop reading. Turn off the news and get in the pews! You have the right to bask in the presence of the One who offers you His strength and courage to face every day.

A Taste of Faithfulness

Lord, help me to realize that You are my Source of Strength and peace in this world of chaos and fear. Amen.

Picking the Fruit

But what happens when we live God's way? He brings gifts into our lives, much the same way that fruit appears in an orchard—things like affection for others, exuberance about life, serenity. We develop a willingness to stick with things, a sense of compassion in the heart, and a conviction that a basic holiness permeates things and people. We find ourselves involved in loyal commitments, not needing to force our way in life, able to marshal and direct our energies wisely.

Galatians 5:22-23 THE MESSAGE

This version of Galatians gives us a little deeper understanding of what the gifts of the Spirit are really about. It gives us a desire to start picking more fruit so that we can be filled with more and more of these wonderful things. The gifts are available to us and our desire for them helps us to discover them.

Consider the gifts you already have and see if there are still some that you would like to have. If you discover a gift that is not yet fully developed in you, then focus your energy on it today.

Let God create that gift in you.

A Taste of the Spirit

Lord, help me climb a little higher, work a little harder, and be ready to accept the gifts of Your Spirit. Amen.

Fruit du Jour

"I appointed you to go and produce fruit that will last, so that the Father will give you whatever you ask for, using My name."

John 15:16 NLT

The fruit of the Spirit is indeed fruit that will last forever. It will grow with you, shape you, and help you become more than you would have ever been before.

John Blanchard asked, "How often do we need to see God's face, hear His voice, feel His touch, know His power? The answer to all these questions is the same: Every day!"

When you live by the Spirit, you see God's face more clearly, hear His voice more often, and feel His unlimited power in your life. You need His touch every day. Ask for anything in His name and He'll see that you get it. He wants you to produce the fruit that will last.

A Taste of the Spirit

Lord, You have given me so many gifts and I glorify Your name for all that You do for me. Help me to be wise and honor the gifts You have given me. Amen.

Destiny Awaits!

*When a potter makes jars out of clay, doesn't he have
the right to use the same lump of clay to make one jar
for decoration and another to throw garbage into?*

Romans 9:21 NLT

It's not always easy to remember that you are not
the Potter, but simply the clay that can be used by
God in any way He chooses. He clearly needs us to
do different things to help make it possible for all to
come to Him in time. If you give Him the right to
mold you, you'll discover that He has something
beautiful in mind for you.

Take a moment and imagine a loving Potter who
enjoys shaping your life at this very moment. See
Him looking at you with great interest, making certain that you will be perfectly set for the work He
has for you. Though He may have created other
wonderful pieces of pottery to do other jobs, you
are unique, the only one with His fingerprint. You
were designed for great things.

A Taste of Goodness

Lord, help me to become all that You intended for me
to become. Let me be a labor of love, a joy to Your Spirit. Amen.

Are You Determined to Meet Your Goals?

Take a lesson from the ants, you lazybones. Learn from their ways and be wise! Even though they have no prince, governor, or ruler to make them work, they labor hard all summer, gathering food for the winter.

Proverbs 6:6 NLT

It's easy to get side-tracked. A friend needs your help, your kids get sick, or a thousand other things call for your attention. As you take care of these things, others are neglected.

Having a plan is a good thing and it helps to guide your steps. If you can see where you want to go in your mind's eye, it's a lot easier to get there.

I'm sure you've seen how ants build their houses and lug food and things three times their size from one spot to another. Their goal is to get ready for winter and they don't stop until nature shuts the door on their well-prepared nest. When you're determined to meet your goals, nothing can really stop you. Getting side-tracked doesn't need to get you off track. Just keep at it.

A Taste of Determination

Lord, I do sometimes seem to get side-tracked from the things that are most important. Help me to stay on the path, working toward my goals. Amen.

Producing Good Fruit

"A good tree can't produce bad fruit, and a bad tree can't produce good fruit. A tree is identified by the kind of fruit it produces. Figs never grow on thorn bushes or grapes on bramble bushes. A good person produces good deeds from a good heart."

Luke 6:43-45 NLT

Who and what we are has a lot to do with what goes on in our hearts. We say that someone is good-hearted when they give selflessly to the well-being of those around them. Their work is directly influenced by what they believe. In fact, everything they do is closely tied to the discipline of their hearts.

Challenge yourself today to produce even more fruit according to the gifts God has given you. See if there is one place that you might offer the fruit of the Spirit that you may have overlooked before. Keep growing, keep producing and keep sharing with others.

A Taste of Goodness

Lord, let me share the good things that You have given me today. Remind me of those places that I have overlooked and give me an opportunity to plant new seeds of love. Amen.

Go in Peace

*"God blesses those who work for peace,
for they will be called the children of God."*

Matthew 5:9 NLT

As beautiful as it is to feel God's peace in your heart, there is a special blessing for those who work toward establishing peace in the world. Working for peace has become a much more relevant pursuit in the world today since we live in a volatile society and many live in fear and anxiety.

You can be the peacekeeper in your own home, or in your workplace. You can be the voice of reason when conflict arises. You can pray for the good of everyone you know so that their lives have greater peace.

Open the door for peace to enter into your heart, your home and your community. It will make a difference and God will bless you for all that you do as His child.

A Taste of Peace

Lord, help me to be a leader in bringing about peace in the circumstances around me. Help me to offer Your peace to all those I meet. Amen.

Be the Light

*"You are the light of the world – like a city
on a mountain, glowing in the night for all
to see. Don't hide your light under a basket!
Instead, put it on a stand and let it shine for all."*
Matthew 5:14-15 NLT

How can you shine more effectively for God? Have you dimmed your light so much that those around you can't see it shining? If so, it's time to come out from hiding and shine that light for all to see.

You can be the light in many wonderful ways. Every time you offer a smile and a kind word to someone, you're the light. Every time you have compassion on your neighbor or even a stranger, you're the light. Every time you do something as the hands and feet of Christ, you're the light.

Your prayers are like stars that shine and illuminate the way for all those you have offered up to God. Every time you pray, the light shines. Make sure your light is strong and bright today.

A Taste of Kindness

Lord, help me to shine Your light as brightly as I can today. Let me be the light of kindness, of friendship and of compassion every chance I get. Amen.

Hold Fast to the Good

Prove all things; hold fast that which is good.
1 Thessalonians 5:21 KJV

Have you ever had something really good just slip right out of your hands? When that happens, it brings a flood of pain.

Sometimes being able to hold fast to good things simply requires that you identify and list these things in your mind and heart. You lose out when you never even identify the good things you have to begin with. You never gave God credit for giving you something so wonderful.

Make it your business today to think about all the good things God has given you. Write them down and give Him praise for each thing on your list. Thank Him for the joy that you receive from these good things. Hold fast to His goodness so that you take nothing for granted. Thank Him for the amazing good He has done for you.

A Taste of the Good

Lord, thank You for loving me so much and providing me with many good things in life. Amen.

Don't Drop Out!

My dear child, don't shrug off God's discipline, but don't be crushed by it either. It's the child He loves that He disciplines; the child He embraces, He also corrects. God is educating you; that's why you must never drop out.
Hebrews 12:6 THE MESSAGE

Have you ever felt like running away and starting your life all over? Maybe you feel that God always seems to think that you need to learn another lesson, while everyone else seems to coast through His school of learning. Sometimes it's hard to see the big picture and to appreciate the idea that you alone need more discipline.

The truth is that when we enroll in God's school, we become part of His education system with His perks as well as His discipline. The good news is that He cares so much about your well-being that He won't let you move ahead until you're ready.

Don't give up or drop out! You're a great student and God just wants you to be everything He intended you to be.

A Taste of Self-control

Lord, help me today to be ready to learn, grow and accept the work in front of me. Thanks for being such a divine Teacher! Amen.

Be Cheerful All the Time!

Be cheerful no matter what; pray all the time; thank
God no matter what happens. This is the way
God wants you who belong to Christ Jesus to live.
1 Thessalonians 5:16 THE MESSAGE

The idea of being cheerful all the time seems a bit daunting. Even if you have a great disposition most of the time, it would be incredible to be cheerful *all* the time *no matter* what happens.

How is it possible then to do what this verse asks? The answer lies in realizing that being cheerful is the way God wants you to be because you belong to Christ Jesus. Regardless of what happens, you are a child of God, and that means you have every reason to cheer. No matter what your circumstances are, you can cheer, because God is in control.

Now you understand how you can have a reason to be cheerful all the time. You may not be happy about each detail of your life, but you can always be happy in Jesus.

A Taste of Joy

Lord, help me to surrender the details of living on earth to You and embrace the joy of living in Jesus. Amen.

Keep Growing!

But good people will grow like palm trees; they will
be tall like the cedars of Lebanon. Like trees planted
in the Temple of the LORD*, they will grow strong*
in the courtyards of our God. When they are old, they
will still produce fruit; they will be healthy and fresh.

Psalm 92:12-14 NCV

Living in the fruit of the Spirit means that you
nourish yourself in the richness of the Word and
replenish your faithfulness through prayer and
thanksgiving.

Be aware of what you plant, so that you can reap
the good of what you sow. As long as you remain in
the presence of the Spirit, you will be blessed with
renewed strength. You will grow in beauty of heart,
mind and soul.

God loves you, nurtures you and wants you to
grow stronger each day. Feel His blessing on your
life and give thanks for the tender care you receive.

A Taste of Blessing

Dear Lord, thank You for nurturing me in Your garden.
I ask that I might grow in Your love and draw strength
from Your presence each day of my life. Amen.

Love Forgives

Hatred stirs up trouble, but love forgives all wrongs.
Proverbs 10:12 NCV

Forgiveness can be a sticky issue. We're all grateful when God forgives us, but it's not so much fun when we have to forgive someone else. It's even less fun when we don't even recognize the need to ask for forgiveness. It is only when we see the huge log in our own eye that our pride is humbled and we see our need to ask for forgiveness.

Saying "I'm sorry" is hard. Meaning it can be even harder. Learn what you can from an experience and then move on. Holding on to the wrong deed only stirs up trouble.

Love forgives all wrongs, sometimes even without apologies. Love puts all wrongs at the cross of Christ and leaves them there. That's loving and forgiving at its best.

A Taste of Gentleness

Lord, help me surrender any feelings of anger that I may be carrying from past deeds caused by someone toward me or caused by me toward someone else. Let me learn to be truly forgiving out of love for You. Amen.

Dare to Dream ... Dare to Ask!

*"You can ask for anything in My name, and I will
do it, because the work of the Son brings glory to the
Father. Yes, ask anything in My name, and I will do it!"*
John 14:13-14 NLT

What do you dream and hope for and fear all at the
same time? It is important to be a lover of dreams
for that is what fills the heart with joy and expectation. It's important to be a lover of prayer for the
same reason. Prayer puts a foundation under your
dreams and puts them in direct alignment with God.
Ask Him to line your heart up with the dreams He's
given you so that you can work together to create
the vision. God will fulfill the desires of your heart.

Sometimes we dream, sometimes we pray, but
often we forget to put our dreams in the Creator's
hands so He can help us manifest them according
to His will and purpose for us. Ask for your heart's
desires in Jesus' name!

A Taste of Faithfulness

Lord, sometimes I don't lay my dreams before You.
I guess I'm afraid that You won't want them to come
true. Help me to seek Your wisdom in all that I do and
to only desire Your path for my life. Amen.

Prudent Pruning

"I am the true vine, and My Father is the Gardener. He cuts off every branch that doesn't produce fruit, and He prunes the branches that do bear fruit so they will produce even more."
John 15:1-2 NLT

Pruning bushes or trimming the hedges is not easy work. You usually come back worn out from the experience and your newly trimmed shrubs don't even look all that good. However, after a few days, they grow more beautiful and you see the fruit of your labors. You've been a good gardener.

Sometimes, the Heavenly Gardener feels the same about you. He knows that you might not like it if He trims off some old habits, or He weeds out some old friends. He knows you might sulk a bit, but with time, He knows that you'll be more beautiful and fruitful than ever.

With a little of His prudent pruning, you'll be amazed at your own growth.

A Taste of Faithfulness
Lord, it's not easy for me to understand when You trim and prune me. Help me trust my life to Your care in every way and in all I do. Amen.

Live in Harmony

When others are happy, be happy with them. If they are
sad, share their sorrow. Live in harmony with each other.
Romans 12:15-16 NLT

Empathy is the desire and the willingness to be
there for others in their time of emotional need.
Feeling their pain in your heart and in your mind is
a way of deeply understanding what they are going
through. It's a way of motivating yourself to reach
out and offer support.

Some people are naturally empathetic and you
usually can recognize them as the ones who easily
cry at movies or smile at speakers. Others prefer to
insulate themselves from either tears or laughter.

Do you practice empathy? Do you willingly
share your heart and your spirit with those around
you and create greater harmony in the process? God
wants you to live in harmony with all your brothers
and sisters. When you reach out with your hands,
be sure your heart reaches out as well.

A Taste of Gentleness

Lord, it is truly an honor to share in the joy and the sorrows of others. Bless those times in my life when I strive
to bring harmony and love to any situation. Amen.

Enjoy Yourself!

The best that people can do is eat, drink, and enjoy their work. I saw that even this comes from God, because no one can eat or enjoy life without Him.

Ecclesiastes 2:24 NCV

Imagine that you have spent a whole day cleaning, cooking, and setting a lovely table for your family. Now suppose that they come home and no one even notices all your effort and hard work. Not a word of thanks is uttered and you're dumbfounded.

Imagine now that God prepared unique treasures that would give you the greatest joy and spread them before you. Then you came to dinner, hardly ate and walked off without so much as a nod in His direction. His joy and yours would both be destroyed.

Today, make it clear to God that you love all that He does for you and show Him by simply enjoying yourself amidst the many treasures He's created just for you. Give Him your heartfelt thanks and praise!

A Taste of Joy

Lord, sometimes I do forget to thank You for the many treasures You've given me. I am so grateful, Father, for all the gifts You've given me to enjoy. Amen.

Wealth or Riches?

Command those who are rich with things of this world
not to be proud. Tell them to hope in God, not in
their uncertain riches. God richly gives us everything
to enjoy. Tell the rich people to do good, to be rich in
doing good deeds, to be generous and ready to share.

1 Timothy 6:17-18 NCV

In God's sight, there's a big difference between wealthy people and rich people. Wealthy people generally have accumulated more of this world's goods. Rich people have accumulated more ways of doing good and more generous deeds of the heart.

All of us can be rich beyond our wildest dreams. It has nothing to do with the size of our bank accounts, but with the size of our spirits and our hearts. It has to do with how much good we're willing to do. Those good deeds bring true richness to our life experience.

Regardless of your income level, you can be rich any time you choose to be. Give God the glory!

A Taste of Goodness

Lord, bless me with the kind of richness that is open to new experiences, gives generously from the heart, and prays constantly for those in need. Amen.

A New Wrinkle

*Whatever you do, work at it with all your
heart, as working for the Lord, not for men.*
Colossians 3:23

When you work with an enthusiastic person she
makes her job seem interesting and exciting. She
brings a spirit of joy to the work that has nothing
to do with how much she is being paid. She simply
works as though God Himself is her boss.

It's good to learn from such people. Sometimes
as we get older, we lose youthful enthusiasm and
with every wrinkle comes another reason to give up
or to give in to cynicism. But losing enthusiasm does
more than wrinkle the skin, it wrinkles the soul.

Make this an enthusiastic day! Work with all
your heart for the living Lord and honor Him in all
that you do. Offer praise to Him for the great work
He has given you to do. Your enthusiasm will light
up the place and you'll find your spirit soaring.

A Taste of Joy

Lord, renew my spirit for the work I do and help me to
do it in joy for You and in harmony with those around
me. Bless this day according to Your will and purpose.
Amen.

Take Care of the Earth!

God created human beings. God blessed them:
"Prosper! Reproduce! Fill Earth! Take charge!
Be responsible for fish in the sea and birds in the air, for
every living thing that moves on the face of Earth."
Genesis 1:27-28 THE MESSAGE

In a world that is ever shrinking, we witness the demise of our planet. Sometimes we express concern, other times we see it as someone else's job.

Yet, God commanded us in the very beginning to take care of creation. He made all of it to sustain us for many generations and yet, today we realize things are going wrong. Natural disasters have become the order of the day. What can we do to take care of the planet God designed for us to live on?

As Christians, we signed on to be caretakers and to protect each other and the planet God gave us. Thank God today for clean water and a breath of fresh air. Pray for your homeland ... the planet Earth.

A *Taste of Faithfulness*
Lord, help me be faithful to You in the ways I take care of the earth. Increase my understanding of how I can be of service. Amen.

June

God Makes Things Grow

*So neither he who plants nor he who waters
is anything; but only God, who makes things grow.*
1 Corinthians 3:7

What are your ideal conditions for growth? Do you require a lot of attention, good food, light? Whatever you need is available. It was created and provided for you by God long before you were born.

Now that you've been nurtured in His care and branched out on your own, you need to consider where you've been planted. Are your roots deeply established or are you waiting to be transplanted? Be prepared to grow when God creates the perfect mix of sunshine and rain in your life.

As much as we want to avoid clouds and rain, both are necessary to make a rainbow. Today, consider all that you have and where you are. Ask God to guide, renew and refresh your spirit so that you can grow more fully in the light of His love.

A Taste of Patience
Lord, help me to wait patiently for Your direction. Plant my spirit so firmly in You that my only desire is to grow according to Your plan for my life. Amen.

JUNE 2

Follow the Leader

Follow my example, as I follow the example of Christ.
1 Corinthians 11:1

Do you remember when you were little and you played a game called "Follow the leader"? You stood in a line and whatever the person in front did, you did too. It was fun and usually every one had a chance to be the leader for a while.

You are at the head of the line again. You have a chance to be the leader. Follow Christ, and set an example for those who come after you. You can inspire them by speaking words of comfort and love. You can inspire their hearts each time you lend a hand to answer a need or reach out to heal a broken soul.

You're a leader and for some people, you're the only Bible they'll ever read. You're the only example of Christ they'll ever see. What will you show them? How will they learn of His love, His saving grace, His forgiveness? What will they learn from you?

A Taste of Faithfulness

Dear Lord, help me to be a good example to those around me. Let me share the heart and the hope of Jesus Christ with others. Amen.

Spiritless Exercise

*Let us run with endurance the race that God
has set before us. We do this by keeping our eyes on Jesus,
on whom our faith depends from start to finish.*
Hebrews 12:1-2 NLT

We want to run the race as best we can and therefore we have to remember the goal. The goal is to strengthen our faith to endure until the end.

Sometimes people limit their exercise routine to jumping to conclusions, running up bills, stretching the truth, or bending over backwards. Some exercise their rights to side-step responsibility. Others prefer to push their luck. These are spiritless exercises. Obstacles trip them and they have trouble getting up again.

Your faith requires you to exercise your joy in Jesus. You need to run with Him beside you, and step up the pace when He calls you. Exercise is good for you. Exercising your faith in Jesus is even better. Get moving.

A *Taste of Faithfulness*
Lord, help me to run with You, not around You or ahead of You. Help me to get in shape so that I can win the race that You have set before me. Amen.

Stop Asking Why

*Trust in the LORD with all your heart; do not depend
on your own understanding. Seek His will
in all you do, and He will direct your paths.*

Proverbs 3:5-6 NLT

When you first started to talk as a child, you probably began by imitating sounds and saying familiar
words. After that, you started exploring the world
and asked many "why" questions.

When you're in discovery mode, asking why can
help you find the answers you're seeking. But it can
also be confusing when your search results in more
questions. The road to discovery can lead you on a
winding pathway. Sometimes you'll find the truth
waiting for you and other times it will elude you.

Keep your eyes on Jesus and He will direct you
on the right path. Why? Because He loves you and
paved the way for your salvation.

A Taste of Faithfulness

Lord, help me to seek Your will with each step I take.
Forgive me when I smugly feel that I have all the answers. Always keep me on the path You want me to
take. Amen.

Stand for Something or Fall for Anything

"If you do not stand firm in your faith,
you will not stand at all."
Isaiah 7:9

We live in a cause oriented world. You're expected to support everything from cancer research to human rights. Sometimes you're not even sure what a certain "cause" is about.

Fortunately, your faith is not that confusing. You don't need to try to understand complex issues before you can decide whether to become involved or not. Faith is simple and direct. It's about Jesus! When you know what you believe, you stand firm and won't fall.

God wants to give you a ticket home. He's already done everything, you simply have to join Him on the trip. The best part is that it's free. Jesus paid the price for you on Calvary.

Stand up for your faith and enjoy the ride.

A Taste of Faithfulness
Lord, thank You for setting me free in the truth of Jesus. Help me to stand for You in all the things I do today. Amen.

JUNE 6

The Gift of Jesus

Thank God for His Son – a gift too wonderful for words!
2 Corinthians 9:15 NLT

When you've grown up as a Christian and you understand John 3:16, you sometimes forget to meditate on what the gift of Jesus really means. No other
relationship will ever be as important as this one.

How have we dealt with this wonderful gift? We
have adored Him and made Him an important part
of our daily lives and have been grateful for the gift
of His love. Some of us have kept Him somewhere
near, but can't actually remember the last time we
nurtured the relationship. A few of us have received
Him at some point and then put Him away until we
had time to consider His gift later.

You have a gift in God's Son that is too wonderful for words. Meditate on what He means to you
today.

A Taste of Faithfulness
Lord, thank You for Your Son and the gift of His grace,
love and salvation. Draw me closer to You in all that I
do today. Amen.

It's All Possible

*Jesus looked at them intently and said, "Humanly speaking,
it is impossible. But with God everything is possible."*
Matthew 19:26 NLT

Do you ever find yourself running out of possibility
thinking? Your hopes are deflated and you're not
sure what to expect anymore or whether anything is
going to happen that you've been praying for.

When we review past experiences, we prove to
ourselves that most things just aren't possible. But
what's possible for you today depends on your attitude, your gratitude and your willingness to connect with the God of the possible.

If you're not walking intimately with God, you
may not notice possibilities. Plug in to the Source
today and find out what He really wants for you.
You don't have to go it alone. It's always better to
have a strong companion. Are you ready to fulfill
your dreams?

A Taste of Patience

Lord, I admit that I am impatient when waiting for
something good to happen in my life. Help me to be
patient and to see Your possibilities for me. Amen.

Soul Searching

Search all of history, from the time God created
people on the earth until now. See if anything
as great as this has ever happened before.
Deuteronomy 4:32 NLT

It seems fair to say that we spend our lives searching for God. Sometimes we're blessed with great moments when our souls are filled with His joy and all that He has done for us. His presence creates great joy.

We long to remain in constant connection with God. The winding road of life however, causes our relationship with God to fluctuate. When you seek Him with your whole heart, He will be found. Each time you make the connection with God again, your soul is renewed by joy.

Soul searching is a worthy way to spend your time. Keep discovering the mystery, the passion, and the joy that comes from knowing God and walking with Him each day.

A Taste of Faithfulness
Lord, thank You for helping me to discover new joys in You each time I draw close to You. Amen.

A Little Bit of Heaven

Let heaven and earth praise Him,
the seas and all that move in them.
Psalm 69:34

Dwight L. Moody said, "A little faith will bring your soul to heaven, but a lot of faith will bring heaven to your soul."

Do you know the things that give you a "little bit of heaven"? Sometimes it's sitting in a lawn chair on a beautiful day with billowy clouds and calm winds or getting the whole family together and making your favorite feast.

Whatever creates a touch of heaven in your life is a gentle reminder of God's love for you and the joy He wants you to have. Your faith aligns you with Him and your trust in Him makes moments of joy come around more often.

Stop for a moment and offer your heartfelt thanks and praise to God.

A Taste of Joy
Lord, thank You for blessing me with so many wonderful moments to enjoy. Thank You for quiet times and fun times with family and friends. Amen.

A Few Good Deeds

As the body without the spirit is dead,
so faith without deeds is dead.

James 2:26

If you're an artist, you paint. If you're a writer, you put your thoughts into print. If you're a Christian, you tell others of your love for God. Whatever you are, you must fulfill the passions of your heart.

Whenever we are passionate about something, we are enthusiastic about it. We think about it most of the time and try to learn more about it every chance we get. When your spirits are low, you can't experience the passion that lives within you.

What will revive your spirit and make the passion come alive again? It's simple. It's a matter of doing good to others, becoming closely connected to the Spirit of God and coming back to life. In Him is life and that life is yours any time you call His name.

A Taste of Faithfulness

Lord, help me to connect to You today in ways that will revitalize my spirit and renew my energy and strength. Let me share my love for You with those I meet. Amen.

Expressions of Love

*The only thing that counts is faith
expressing itself through love.*
Galatians 5:6

How do you express your love for others? Are you the one who comes up with special treats like freshly baked brownies or an outing to the movies? Maybe you're always there when need arises, and the last one to leave when you've been called to lend a hand.

You share love in a variety of ways. You send greeting cards, offer smiles and hugs, or pray for those you care about.

God is love and His intention is for us to share His love in every way possible. He wants us to show the world what it means to truly love and to live as examples of that great love.

Because love is the fruit of the Spirit, you are called to love yourself, love humanity, and love God's world. May the sweet aroma of His love ripen into great joy for you.

A Taste of Love

Lord, it's not always easy to express Your love to everyone I know. Help me to love each one as You would have me do. Amen.

JUNE 12

Cleaning Up Your Heart

Create in me a pure heart, O God,
and renew a steadfast spirit within me.
Psalm 51:10

Every now and then it's a good idea to take a little personal inventory. You might want to check that you are still on the right track. Are you praising God with your whole heart? Are you willing to teach and share, or offer a kind word when necessary?

Most of us need to do some cleaning-up now and then. We need to vacuum out the spider webs of doubt or unbelief in our lives. We need to toss out a few old ideas and replace them with some fresh insights. We need to love God with our whole hearts, minds, and spirits and love our neighbors as ourselves.

Today, do a little dusting and cleaning. Let go of things that hold you back from loving others as much as you know you can and make room for more of God's Spirit to live within you.

A Taste of the Spirit
Lord, help me get rid of those thoughts and ideas that are not serving me today and replace them with Your gentle Spirit of love. Amen.

The Hungry Lion

Be self-controlled and alert. Your enemy the devil prowls around like a roaring lion looking for someone to devour. Resist him, standing firm in the faith.

1 Peter 5:8-9

Personal demons afflict the best of us and only prayer can drive them away. We may fight to keep our weight under control, to save some money, to keep up with the demands on our lives. We all fight with something, sometimes. Our faith can help us immeasurably in those fights and God offers us strength to overcome great obstacles.

There is surely a battle raging and not everyone recognizes the existence of the enemy. In truth, a hungry lion, the devil, is walking about searching for ways to claim your soul. Stand strong in your faith and refuse to be deceived. Your faith in Christ Jesus is your strength and your shield.

A Taste of Faithfulness
Lord, I feel helpless sometimes in the midst of the battles raging every day. Guard me and protect me in Jesus' name. Amen.

JUNE 14

Seize the Day!

Seize life! Eat bread with gusto, drink wine with a robust heart. Oh yes – God takes pleasure in your pleasure! Dress festively every morning. Don't skimp on colors or scarves. Relish life with the spouse you love each and every day of your precarious life. Each day is God's gift.

Ecclesiastes 9:7-9 THE MESSAGE

We all talk about living life to the fullest. We want to get up every morning filled with enough enthusiasm to give it our all. We want to, but we don't!

Why? Most of us would say because we have to face reality. We have to go to work, to school, raise little children and visit sick friends. The idea of eating our bread with gusto doesn't seem right then!

The teacher in Ecclesiastes had the same issues we have. He too had to face the realities of life. He had to keep trusting in God's love, mercy and grace. Yet, he survived all that and he reminds us that each day is God's gift. We can accept life's challenges with a joyful heart because God is with us each day!

A Taste of Joy

Lord, help me to remember that You meant for me to enjoy life. Bless me today and help me seize the day! Amen.

Honor and Service

So honor the LORD and serve Him wholeheartedly.
Joshua 24:14 NLT

Think of the things you like to do wholeheartedly. Perhaps you like to clean a room and see it come back to life as you dust and straighten shelves and tables. Perhaps you like to tell stories with such enthusiasm that everyone listens. Whatever it is, there are things that you do with your whole heart.

When Jesus commanded us to love God with our whole heart, He intended us to do so with every breath, at every opportunity, and with every service we might render. We do it because we want to honor Him in every possible way. Look at the things you're doing today. See if you can discover the moments that you're truly serving God in all you do.

Awaken your spirit to the gift of serving with a heart of joy. It'll make your whole day brighter.

A Taste of Love

Lord, help me to love You in all that I do. Whether I'm reading or working, let me do it with the joy of knowing that I do it in service to You. Amen.

Certain Treasures

Tell them to do good, to be rich in good deeds,
and to be generous and willing to share.
In this way, they will lay up treasure for themselves
as a firm foundation for the coming age.
1 Timothy 6:18-19

Most of us have more riches than we realize. We may still struggle to pay our bills or keep our kids in college, but our basic needs are pretty much covered.

Timothy addresses a different kind of richness. He's suggesting that the more we do for others, the richer we become. Sharing your heart, your thoughts and your smile might do more for someone than your money.

Store up real treasures for yourself by doing good deeds. You'll discover a new ability to give and share your "wealth" with the world. It will do your heart good.

A Taste of Goodness

Lord, help me to share kindness and goodness always. Let me not withhold good deeds from others. Amen.

A Kind Word

Timely advice is as lovely as golden apples in a silver basket.
Proverbs 25:11 NLT

We sometimes shy away from sharing our hearts when giving advice to our friends. Why? We tell ourselves it's not our business or that they have the right to do what they want. Perhaps we fear being rejected by someone that means a lot to us and we assume it's better to keep quiet.

This proverb is a beautiful reminder that to offer our advice is the most loving thing we can do. If we offer it in kindness, with the intention to help the other person, then it is the right thing. Then we've put beautiful golden thoughts into a silver basket that we may give to someone who needs advice.

Sometimes the Spirit prompts you to offer help. Be prayerful. Be kind. Lovingly share your heart with others and your advice will bear fruit.

A Taste of Kindness
Lord, help me to know the difference between sharing a self-motivated opinion and giving loving advice. Help me to listen for Your direction to give timely, compassionate advice to those who need it. Amen.

What Do You Seek?

"Your heavenly Father already knows all your needs, and He will give you all you need from day to day if you live for Him and make the Kingdom of God your primary concern."
Matthew 6:32-33 NLT

According to Scripture, if you seek God all your needs will be met. If that doesn't seem to be true for you what can you do?

If your heart is focused on God each day, prayerfully aligned with His will, desiring to be led by His Spirit, and joyfully working to build your relationship with Him, then you're seeking the Kingdom.

Sometimes I think I'm seeking the Kingdom, but I'm actually just hoping God will watch over me while I am doing my own thing. I get all my stuff done and only then can I make time for God. I don't think that's the way to seek God. Put your load aside for a while and seek God first. He will help you carry the load.

A Taste of Faithfulness

Lord, I know I get too busy and then I wonder why You aren't there when I'm struggling to get it all done. Be with me today, Lord, because I want to walk with You. Amen.

Fix Your Thoughts

Fix your thoughts on what is true and honorable and right.
Think about things that are pure and lovely and admirable.
Think about things that are excellent and worthy of praise.

Philippians 4:8 NLT

Your thoughts influence your deeds. Your focus will be negative if you constantly think about worries and troubles in the world.

Are you giving yourself a chance to think about the good things? Do you spend time praising God for those things that make your life good? Do you thank Him for your family, work, friends, and the food on your table? Do you consider the love God has for you?

Think about those things! Allow yourself to experience the joy of knowing you are a child of God. Live as a child of God by fixing your thoughts on things above. Go on! Put a flower in your lapel today and remind yourself that every good gift comes from above.

A Taste of Gentleness

Father, help me to remember that You have lavished great gifts on me. Help me to see them and share them with others. Amen.

No Worries

Don't worry about anything; instead, pray about everything.
Tell God what you need, and thank Him for all He has done.
If you do this, you will experience God's peace, which is far
more wonderful than the human mind can understand.

Philippians 4:6-7 NLT

Let's try an experiment. Give yourself permission not to worry for one day. Don't let any worries come near you. If one tries to get in, just slam the door in its face.

Start by telling God about your worries then leave them at His feet. You can't pick them up and carry them again. Once you've handed the worries over, thank God for all He has done for you already.

How did it feel not to worry? With what did you replace your worries and fears? If you were flooded with peace and love, embrace that feeling. If you did it for one day, try it again the next. If you couldn't quite do it for a whole day, practice. Put worry aside and allow grace to enter.

A Taste of Joy

Lord, I know I worry about things that I need to surrender to You. Help me to offer You my concerns, accept Your help, and replace those worries with words of praise. Thank You, Lord. Amen.

When You Can't See Clearly

We live by faith, not by what we see.
2 Corinthians 5:7 CEV

When you're in the habit of living by faith every day, you aren't always concerned about seeing what lies ahead. You leave tomorrow in God's hand and you keep walking, even if you have to walk in the dark.

When you're walking in the dark, you can't see clearly but you can still hear clearly. You can listen to God's voice and seek His direction.

Faith always lets the light in and leads you in the right direction. It moves you closer to God. It dispels the darkness around you so that you can live in the light.

Helen Keller said, "If the blind put their hand in God's, they find their way more surely than those who see but have not faith or purpose." Continue in faith and fulfill the purpose for your life.

A Taste of Faithfulness

Lord, sometimes I am blinded by the trappings of the world. I set my faith aside and trust my intellect. Help me walk closer to You, even in the dark. Amen.

Focus on God

*Can all your worries add a single
moment to your life? Of course not.*
Matthew 6:27 NLT

Regret looks back and plays the "what-if" game.
Worry looks around and tries to solve everything
on its own. Faith looks up because the only Source
of hope is there.

We rely on our conscience to guide us and on our
intellect to make good choices. We think we have
everything under control because we've mapped
out a plan and yet somehow, worry still walks in
and hope loiters far away in the background. Before
we know it neither intellect nor the Spirit is running
things, but worry is!

Today, make it a point not to look back or around,
but joyfully look up to God in faith.

A Taste of Faithfulness
Lord, help me to walk in faith with You today letting
all my worries go, so my heart stays focused on You.
Amen.

Lifting Weights

*Without faith no one can please God.
We must believe that God is real and that
He rewards everyone who searches for Him.*
Hebrews 11:6 CEV

We all want to be healthy. We watch our diet, try to avoid desserts and too many visits to our favorite fast-food chain. We run, jog, go to the gym and we even lift weights. Lifting weights tones our muscles, strengthens our bodies and helps us maintain a healthy body weight.

Faith is important for spiritual health. It lifts you up, strengthens you and enables you to enjoy life more. You shouldn't carry your faith around as an accessory; it should be something that sustains you. It should help you maintain all your connections to God in very real ways.

If you want to lift weights at the gym, go ahead. If you want to lift weights off your life, go to God. He'll carry your burdens. All you have to do is to go to Him in prayer.

A Taste of Faithfulness
Lord, I raise my hands to You and invite You to lift my burdens so that I can enjoy all the good things You bless me with. Amen.

Family Ties

God sets the lonely in families.
Psalm 68:6

Summer is usually the time for big family reunions and other gatherings. Graduations and weddings are joyfully celebrated by families brought together by these occasions.

The globe continues to shrink and we have all become more familiar with the way in which families on other continents and in other cultures live. We're becoming increasingly aware that we are truly more alike than we are different from our neighbors. Everybody seeks love and approval and joy within families.

As children of God, we all have the same Father and we're a family! We can learn to love each other and find mutual joys and gifts to share, or we can become estranged and dysfunctional forgetting our royal blood.

A Taste of Love
Lord, help me to appreciate and love the family You have given me, and so honor Your name in all my relationships. Amen.

Getting a Piece of the Rock

My soul finds rest in God alone; my salvation comes
from Him. He alone is my rock and my salvation;
He is my fortress, I will never be shaken.

Psalm 62:1-2

Do you have someone in your life who is a rock? You know, the person you count on when life gets tough, the person you know will always stand by you. This person is strong for your sake and for others.

A TV commercial might make a certain insurance company seem as solid as a rock, dependable and reliable. I don't know about insurance, but we have assurance through our faith in the One true God. He is your rock and salvation and you can depend on Him. His strength is sure and His victory is certain. If you're seeking a person, place or a thing to keep you forever safe, stop looking. You will only find it in Jesus Christ.

A Taste of the Spirit

Lord, my Rock and my Salvation, thank You for loving me so much and keeping me forever in Your care! Amen.

Rivers of Hope

So I pray that God, who gives you hope, will keep you happy and full of peace as you believe in Him. May you overflow with hope through the power of the Holy Spirit.
Romans 15:13 NLT

Don't you love sitting on a peaceful river bank on a warm, sunny day? Maybe there are a few clouds in the sky. You can close your eyes and hear the crickets chirping and the fish jumping.

When you're not sitting on the river bank and you're following your daily routine, is anything preventing peace from flowing within you? Is your hope choked by weeds and your joy suffocating under layers upon layers of life's problems? Sit back, close your eyes and take five minutes to renew your spirit. God is waiting there to refresh you and give you peace and power through the Holy Spirit.

All you have to do is rest quietly by the Source of living water.

A Taste of Joy
Lord, help me today to rest in Your fountains of joy. Remind me that You are always with me and grant me Your peace. Amen.

Piano Practice, Baseball Practice, Hope Practice

Work hard at whatever you do.
Ecclesiastes 9:10 CEV

We all know that practice makes perfect and that it takes a lot of practice to become good at something special like playing the piano or learning to dance.

The same rule applies to your spiritual life. You may pray and your Bible reading may be quite good, but how good are you at hope practice. When you practice hope daily in a very conscious way, you will discover an amazing thing. Your spirit becomes happier and happier. Hope practice builds your spiritual muscles. Today, be sure to get some hope practice. Come on now, practice, practice, practice!

A Taste of Hope
Lord, let Your Spirit wash over me today and bathe me in peace and hope. Help me to be more aware of the importance of nurturing a hopeful and positive attitude. Amen.

Collecting Your Inheritance

I pray that your hearts will be flooded with light so that you can understand the wonderful future He has promised to those He called. I want you to realize what a rich and glorious inheritance He has given to His people.

Ephesians 1:18 NLT

An inheritance is usually something that someone who loves us has left us in a will. It is set aside to be given to us at the right time. An inheritance helps to sustain our future.

When Jesus left the earth and returned to heaven, He left us an inheritance. He left us a future. He left the greatest future anyone could ever wish for. He left us eternal life. He promised us a place in the Father's house forever.

In order to enjoy your inheritance He also left you with a gift. He gave you the Holy Spirit so that you can have power on earth over evil and can understand His Word. He left you hope and joy and strength to keep you going amidst earthly crises.

A Taste of Joy

Lord, I am so grateful for all that You've done for me, not just today, but in the future as well. Thank You for redeeming my soul. Amen.

From Gloom to Bloom

Some people brought Him [Jesus] a paralyzed man on a mat. Seeing their faith, Jesus said to the paralyzed man, "Take heart, son! Your sins are forgiven."

Matthew 9:2 NLT

Have you ever been gloomy, frightened or paralyzed by fears? Have you struggled with depression and worry? You're not alone.

Friends played a big role in the life of the paralyzed man. They knew in their hearts that Jesus could heal him and that their friend would be able to walk again. Sometimes it takes the faith that comes from those around you to carry you until you can walk on your own again.

If anything is keeping you down today, remember the Lord's words, "Take heart, your sins are forgiven." You are now free to celebrate, move around, jump up and down and rejoice through the grace of God because the clouds are moving. The sun is coming out again and it's time for you to bloom.

A Taste of Joy

Lord, I thank You for the friends who hold me up in prayer and keep me in front of Your throne. I thank You for blessing me and bringing me great joy. Amen.

Make the World a Brighter Place

"When you put on a luncheon or a dinner, invite the poor, the crippled, the lame, and the blind. Then God will reward you for inviting those who could not repay you."
Luke 14:12-14 NLT

Is your heart touched by the needs of suffering people? Do you wonder what you can do?

Martin Luther King, Jr. said, "God is able to make a way out of no way, and transform dark yesterdays into bright tomorrows. This is our hope for becoming better people. This is our mandate for seeking to make a better world."

You're part of God's way to make the world a better place. You might invite the lost and the lame to sit at your table, or you might donate food to your favorite charity. Whatever you prefer to do, do it! Make a difference! Experience God's blessing for helping those who could not possibly repay you.

A Taste of Goodness
Lord, sometimes I take for granted the warm bed I sleep in and the warm meal I enjoy at dinner time. You lavish so much on me. Help me to share all that I have with others. Amen.

July

Grandma's Faith

I have been reminded of your sincere faith, which first lived in your grandmother Lois and in your mother Eunice and, I am persuaded, now lives in you also.

2 Timothy 1:5

A faithful grandmother can be a genuine blessing. My great-grandmother was the one who planted a seed in me that grew into a living faith. She gave me my first Bible and said the first prayers I heard. I was blessed to have known her and I still often think of her.

You don't know what influence you may have on your children or your grandchildren. You may be the one who plants the seed of faith, waters it, or nurtures it into full blossom. You may not see the fruit of your labor of love, but God brings each person to Himself in His own time. He sends people to lead us and explain certain truths.

Today, let's celebrate our grandmothers and those in our lives who have shared their faith and given us hope for tomorrow.

A Taste of Faithfulness

Lord, thank You for mothers and grandmothers and those who have guided us on Your path. Amen.

Place God First

*Dear children, keep away from anything
that might take God's place in your hearts.*
1 John 5:21 NLT

Name the ten most important things in your life. Arrange them in order of importance; the most important being number one. Be honest. Are your children, colleagues and best friend on the list? They should be. God wants to be on your list too. In fact, He must be number one on your list.

A part of you may realize that this is right. It is however an emotional struggle not to put your spouse or children first. God does not want to take away your love for your children, spouse or work. He simply wants to be sure that nothing replaces Him in your life.

Today, as you share your love with your family and friends, take time to honor the One who gave them to you and who only wants the best for you. Give God first place in your heart.

A Taste of Love

Lord, help me to love my family in all the ways You've given me to love. Help me love and worship You above all else. Amen.

Moral Excellence

A life of moral excellence leads to knowing God better. Knowing God leads to self-control. Self-control leads to patient endurance, and patient endurance leads to godliness.
2 Peter 1:5-6 NLT

Defining morality in a world without clearly defined rules has become difficult. We claim to believe in the Commandments, yet find a reasonable excuse to make exceptions to the rules. We still go to war, and hate our brothers in other parts of the world.

Making the right choices will become easier as we get to know God better. When we begin to understand real love and really love our fellowmen, we'll come to terms with what it means to love everyone simply because God created us all.

Not one of us can claim to be perfect, but we can claim Jesus Christ as our Savior and Lover of our souls. Knowing this, we can continually learn from Him and grow in self-control.

A Taste of Self-control

Lord, it is hard to understand some of the moral dilemmas we face today. Help me to live according to Your will and purpose for my life. Amen.

A Future Filled with Hope

"So there is hope for your future," declares the LORD.
Jeremiah 31:17

Henri J. Nouwen said, "Those who keep speaking about the sun while walking under a cloudy sky are messengers of hope, the true saints of our day."

You know people who always go around with some sunny saying on their lips and a smile on their faces no matter what the circumstances are. You appreciate their optimism most of the time, but you wonder if they ever watch the news!

Still, you wish you were more like them. It can't be bad to be more hopeful, more certain that God is with you and that things will work out in the end.

Today is your day to be one of them, one of those joy-filled, optimistic, believers in the Lord who just know He's in control and that He holds the future in His hands. God knows there's hope for your future and He wants you to know it too.

A Taste of Joy

Lord, it does bring me joy to think about a future filled with hope. Renew my hope in the future this day. Amen.

You Can Do It!

When I was really suffering, I prayed to the Lord. He answered my prayer, and took my worries away. The Lord is on my side, and I am not afraid of what others can do to me.
Psalm 118:5-6 CEV

Do you have a dream to pursue and a goal to accomplish? Pray! Align yourself with God's will for you and He will enable you to realize your goals and dreams.

Henry Ford once said, "One of the greatest discoveries a man makes, one of his great surprises, is to find he can do what he was afraid he couldn't do."

Don't wait for someone else's approval, you may wait a long time. If you're waiting for ideal circumstances and conditions, they might never come. If you're unwilling or scared to proceed, pray about it and ask God to help you move forward. Do it for your own sake and for God's glory.

A Taste of Peace
Lord, grant me peace as I move in a new direction in my life. Help me to move forward according to Your timing. Amen.

Being Filled with the Spirit

Be filled with the Spirit. Speak to one another
with psalms, hymns and spiritual songs.
Sing and make music in your heart to the Lord.
Ephesians 5:18-19

Have you experienced a moment lately when you knew without a doubt that the Spirit was moving your heart and soul? You were overcome with the joy of knowing God's love is in you and that you could do nothing but rejoice, sing and pray.

If that's not happened to you lately, it's time to figure out why not. The Spirit is available to you *all* the time and having His Spirit move yours should be a fairly common occurrence.

Stop waiting for an emotional feeling to come over you. Maybe you just need to start offering prayers of thanksgiving and singing spiritual songs to the Lord. When you do that, you're almost guaranteed to have a sense that the Spirit is moving.

Go on! Sing a little and let your spirit dance.

A Taste of the Spirit

Lord, be with me today and hear me as I lift my voice in prayer and praise to You. Move within my being, Lord, and let me walk with You. Amen.

Daily Requirements

"And now, Israel, what does the LORD your God require of you? He requires you to fear Him, to live according to His will, to love and worship Him with all your heart and soul, and to obey the LORD's commands and laws that I am giving you today for your own good."

Deuteronomy 10:12-13 NLT

If you take a supplement every day, you'll get your required daily amount of vitamins and minerals.

This list tells you what you need to do to stay strong and healthy in the Lord. Somehow the words, "for your own good" strike a little fear because usually they imply an unpleasant process. Your mother probably said, "Take this medicine for your own good."

Tell God that you really do want to do the things that are good for you. Surrender your pride, stubbornness and selfishness and step aside from what you think is good. See if you can discover what God thinks is good for you. Take a closer look at His daily requirements.

A Taste of Faithfulness

Lord, I don't always like the things that are meant to be for my good. Sometimes I downright resist them. Help me to seek Your will for my own good today. Amen.

Holy Spirit Fellowship

May the grace of the Lord Jesus Christ, and the love of God, and the fellowship of the Holy Spirit be with you all.
2 Corinthians 13:14

Before starting a new day, be sure to accept God's grace, love, and fellowship. How do you do that?

Accepting His grace means that you accept the forgiveness and mercy that Christ offers you. You then share that forgiveness and mercy and grace with others. You rejoice in knowing how much you have been given and what a great gift it is to you.

Accepting God's love differs from accepting your spouse's love or your mother's love. You realize that you are loved for the person you are. It's believing that you are lovable and deserve to be loved. Thank God for loving you unconditionally.

To accept fellowship with the Holy Spirit means inviting Him to walk with you and share in everything you do or say. It means embracing His friendship and His direction for each step you take today.

Accept all God's great blessings for you!

A Taste of the Spirit

I don't often consider the grace and blessings You give me. Enable me to receive more from You today. Amen.

Forgiveness

How great is God's love for all who worship Him?
Greater than the distance between heaven
and earth! How far has the LORD taken our sins
from us? Further than the distance from east to west!
Psalm 103:11-12 CEV

How easily do you forgive? If you've been injured by someone, do you keep that injury as fresh as possible?

Forgiveness is often puzzling. If we need forgiveness, we want it instantly. Drop in a forgiveness tablet, watch it fizz, presto ... problem solved. That's what we like when we're the ones needing forgiveness.

When we need to forgive someone else it's another matter. We might be bearing that injustice to give us an excuse to stop living, or to not achieve anything important. If we hold a grudge, we're off the hook because we have someone to blame.

Let it go ... you'll be glad you did.

A Taste of Peace
Lord, grant me the willingness to forgive, to accept forgiveness and to let go of past injuries. Help me move forward today in love. Amen.

Try a Little Kindness

You will be well rewarded for saying something kind, but all some people think about is how to be cruel and mean.

Proverbs 13:2 CEV

Are you a joy to be around? Are you apt to say mean things?

Kindness doesn't take more time. It doesn't require a special setting and it doesn't have limits. You can't use up your kindness quotient. You will never find yourself in a position where you have no more kindness left, unless you've forgotten who you belong to. God's Spirit creates a heart of kindness and gentleness and goodness in you. Receive it and share it with others.

Pretend it's National Kindness Day today! Go out there and radiate kindness.

A Taste of Kindness

Lord, it seems so simple to be kind. Yet, it isn't always easy. Fill me with a spirit of kindness. Amen.

Willing to Do what God Wants

*Since we could not get Paul to change his mind,
we gave up and prayed, "Lord, please
make us willing to do what You want."*
Acts 21:14 CEV

Many of us have been saying The Lord's Prayer for years. We say it and we believe it as we end it with "Thy will be done." What does it mean to want God's will to be done?

The Scripture verse from Acts shows us that even the ancients weren't always sure and had to ask God to make them "willing" to do what God wanted. We're no different today. We often have to step back, give up and pray the same prayer. "Lord, please make us willing to do what You want."

When life throws you an unexpected curve, you sometimes wonder whose will is being followed. What is God's will concerning you? Make it a priority to find out. Let God lead you to the place He wants you to be.

A Taste of Faithfulness

Lord, I know that I ask Your guidance in important matters and I strive to do Your will. But help me do what You want in all things. Amen.

Putting On the Armor

Be strong in the Lord and in His mighty power.
Put on the full armor of God so that you can
take your stand against the devil's schemes.
Ephesians 6:10-11

Do you need to go through your closest and give old stuff to charity? Just don't throw out your suit of armor. It's perhaps not quite as shiny as when you first put it on, but still in good repair and capable of doing the job. It may be slightly out of fashion, but not out of style.

You were given that armor for just one reason. It's your protective coating against the prowler who often appears to be harmless, just to catch you off guard. Wearing your armor will keep you standing in God's care. In fact, it's indestructible and was designed with you in mind.

So, get rid of those old shirts from college that you're never going to wear anyway, and let go of those old worn tennis shoes, but never give away your armor. You'll always need it.

A Taste of the Spirit
Lord, protect me as I go into the world today. Keep me strong in Your mighty power. Amen.

Becoming Wise

My child, listen to me and treasure my instructions.
Tune your ears to wisdom, and concentrate on understand-
ing. Cry out for insight and understanding. Search for
them as you would for lost money or hidden treasure.

Proverbs 2:1-4 NLT

Wisdom seems like an old-fashioned word, but it still packs a punch! How do we become wise? Why do we seek wisdom? Most of us act wisely in certain situations but foolish in others. Many of us just go from one day to the next without thinking about whether we make wise choices or not.

It's a new day and a new chance to think about your choices. Consider the reasons why you make certain decisions and pray for wisdom in making those decisions. Try praying about each decision you make for the next twenty-four hours and see if it makes a difference. You'll discover some great treasures and you'll become wise.

A Taste of Wisdom

Lord, grant me greater insight and understanding about the choices I make. Create in me a desire to be wise. Amen.

Life's Windstorms

They went to Jesus and woke him up, "Master, Master!
We are about to drown!" Jesus got up and ordered the wind
and waves to stop. They obeyed, and everything was calm.
Then Jesus asked the disciples, "Don't you have any faith?"

Luke 8:23-25 CEV

If you've ever been in a storm where you feared for
your life, you can understand the disciples' concerns
here. Recently I flew to Ohio. A woman with a tiny
baby sat next to me. As I was looking at my companion to tell her what a cute baby she had, I saw a
flash of light and the plane suddenly dropped. I'm
pretty sure we had been struck by lightening. Everyone was upset and afraid. I prayed.

About twenty minutes later, the captain told us
he didn't expect any further experiences like the
one we just had. He never told us what happened,
but I know it was Jesus who kept me calm.

I believed all the passengers were meant to get
home safe and sound. Having faith to get through
storms isn't easy, but it is essential.

A Taste of Peace
Lord, be with me and calm the stormy winds of life today. Amen.

May All Go Well With Your Soul

*Dear friend, I pray that you may enjoy good
health and that all may go well with you,
even as your soul is getting along well.*
3 John 2

The most important aspect of John's wish is the prayer that things will go well with your soul. You can have a healthy body, a healthy mind and healthy relationships, yet struggle with an unhealthy soul.

What do you wish for your neighbors and friends today? You may hope that they are well or pray that God watches over them. You could also say, "May things be well with your soul." When things are well with your soul, you are at peace. When you are at peace, you experience happier relationships. When you're happy in your relationships, you feel healthier.

May things go well with your soul.

A Taste of the Spirit
Lord, may Your peace flood through me like a river today and bring joy to my soul. Amen.

Graceful Oaks

The LORD has planted them like strong
and graceful oaks for His own glory.
Isaiah 61:3 NLT

Don't you just love trees in summer? They are so majestic and commanding and they offer you their leafy, green shade free of charge. They bend in the breeze without breaking and they provide shelter for living creatures.

Like the mighty oaks, God planted us in His garden. He put us there to care for all the living things that are part of it. He placed us there for His glory.

Consider the part you play in the garden where you are planted. Are you the mighty oak that offers strength, support and shade for those who pass by? Or are you the maple sapling that shares its sweetness each spring? Perhaps you're the one who weeds out the things that don't belong there.

You've been placed in the garden for God's glory. What will you do for Him today?

A Taste of Goodness
Lord, help me to grow stronger in Your light and share Your goodness with those I meet today. Amen.

Compassionate Samaritan

*"Then a despised Samaritan came along,
and when he saw the man, he felt deep pity."*
Luke 10:33 NLT

Compassion is noteworthy today because we don't expect it. It's even more surprising when we see compassion coming from someone we've determined to be inferior because of race, creed, or some other arbitrary measure.

The story about the Samaritan is such an example. Each one of us can be placed in a labeled box representing characteristics that others may despise. We belong to the wrong religion, race, or we live on the wrong side of town. Whatever it is, some people feel justified to walk past those in need simply because they don't fit their description of someone worthy of their compassion.

You have a Samaritan heart. You have the kind of compassion that warms the lives of others wherever you go. Be thankful that God has given you this gift.

A Taste of Compassion
Lord, help me to have more compassion on all of Your children wherever I find them today. Amen.

The Friendship Factor

*There was an immediate bond of love between
them, and they became the best of friends.*
1 Samuel 18:1 NLT

Friendships are formed in various ways. Sometimes
you click with someone from the word go. You meet
someone for the first time and they automatically
become part of your life from that moment on. You
feel as if you've known them for a very long time.

C. S. Lewis said, "Friendship is born at that moment when one person says to another, 'What? You
too? I thought I was the only one!'" It's important
for us to have people in our lives we can relate to or
who seem to understand our goals and our hearts'
desires. Those are the people who sustain us in all
circumstances.

Today is a good day to honor your friendships.
Thank God for each person in your life who makes
a continual difference to your well-being in an act
of love.

A Taste of Love

Lord, I thank You for my dear friends and even the ac-
quaintances who support me, lend a helping hand and
encourage me to follow my dreams. Amen.

When the Light Goes Out

So once again, I, the LORD All-Powerful tell you, "See that justice is done and be kind and merciful to one another!"
Zechariah 7:9 CEV

Our life's journey takes us along many windy roads and we often find ourselves sitting in momentary darkness, feeling uncertain about which way to go.

Albert Schweitzer said, "Sometimes our light goes out but is blown into flame by another human being. Each of us owes deepest thanks to those who have rekindled this light."

When the light goes out for us, we should trust God to sustain us and rely on friends to help us find the light again. Remember that wherever we go today, we may come across someone in that very place. Someone sitting in the dark may be waiting for you to lead them to the light again.

Ask God to show you people who need the light of kindness. We're all on this journey together.

A Taste of Kindness
Lord, when my light goes out, I am grateful for others who help me find my way again. Make me aware of any kindness I can offer to someone else as well. Amen.

Love is Such a Good Thing!

Love each other with genuine affection,
and take delight in honoring each other.
Romans 12:10 NLT

Most of us are loving in gentle and kind ways. But, sometimes, we need to be more enthusiastic. We need to embrace the people in our lives and let them know without a doubt how much they are loved. We need to share our love and God's love more fully.

Jeremy Taylor said, "The more we love, the better we are; and the greater our friendships are, the dearer we are to God." We need to get out there and be better at sharing our love with one another.

Perhaps your friends and family might think you have gone over the edge if you're this enthusiastic. Or they might find it wonderfully refreshing and be delighted in the special love you share. It could be worth a try!

A Taste of Love

Lord, I know that I'm often too reserved to show the love I feel for my friends and family. Enable me to share my heart and Your love with them today. Amen.

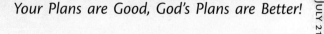
Your Plans are Good, God's Plans are Better!

*Be glad for all God is planning for you. Be patient
in trouble, and always be prayerful. When God's
children are in need, be the one to help them out.*

Romans 12:12-13 NLT

It's always a good thing to plan ahead. Then you move ahead with more confidence and you're ready to cope with unexpected setbacks.

However skilled we are, it's important to remember that even though our plans may be good, God's plans are better! When we decided to follow God, we declared ourselves willing to serve in whatever way He wants. It might mean inviting unexpected guests for dinner or giving more than you thought you'd have to in a crisis to offset the immediate needs of another.

Each day we need to have plans. Then, we need to surrender those plans to the will of our Heavenly Father. He is the only One who can see the big picture and knows everyone's needs. Surrender your plans to Him today.

A Taste of Patience

Lord, I trust You to work out Your plans in my life so that I can be a blessing to others. Amen.

Being Fruitful

*"I am the vine, and you are the branches.
If any stay joined to Me, and I stay joined
to you, then you will produce lots of fruit."*

John 15:5 CEV

Producing fruit is a lofty goal and all of us hope we're doing so. There are lots of ways to be fruitful. We can be fruitful with our time, money, or with our generosity. We can be fruitful with our prayers, kindness, or our spirits.

You're a branch of the True Vine. Whatever you do to produce fruit reflects on your connection to that vine. You must consider every act, every deed, every prayer as an attempt to produce fruit for the good of the Kingdom.

Draw up a To-Do list and check to see if any of your efforts can produce more fruit for the Vine-dresser today.

A Taste of Fruitfulness

Lord, I seem to be busy in hundreds of ways. I don't always stop to see if the things on my list are producing fruit for the Kingdom. Keep me mindful of You today. Amen.

A Garden of Goodness

Their life will be like a watered garden,
and all their sorrows will be gone.
Jeremiah 31:12 NLT

Most of us love gardens in summertime. We imagine plants coming up, producing mouth-watering tomatoes, corn on the cob and herbs of all kinds.

Jeremiah talks about life as a watered garden. Water gives life and nourishes the soil. Enough water and sunshine insure that the garden will produce great bounty and feed its caretaker in return.

Your heart is like a garden from which life, wisdom and goodness come. It's the place where simple joys have meaning and the place that welcomes what life brings, balancing the rain and the sunshine. Is your heart a well-watered garden? Is it nourishing you and refreshing your spirit? If it isn't, see if there are things that need to be hoed out, so you can start growing again.

A Taste of Goodness
Lord, help me to grow in You and nurture those in my care according to Your design for our lives. Amen.

A Giving Heart

You must each make up your own mind as to how much you should give. Don't give reluctantly or in response to pressure. For God loves the person who gives cheerfully.

2 Corinthians 9:7 NLT

We must each define for ourselves what it means to be a giver. We can give our time, our money, or whatever assets we have to share. Whatever we give should be given with a cheerful heart.

When you give because you are passionate about a particular cause or work then it's truly a gift. However, if the collection basket is being passed and you're not sure you even have enough money to buy food, you need to consider whether this is the right time for you to give.

Try to be honest about how and when and what you give. Giving is a matter of heart and mind and capability. You have a right to decide when it's good for you to give.

A Taste of Compassion

Lord, I always want to give, but sometimes I truly don't feel I can. Please help me to be cheerful and honest when I choose to give. Amen.

God At Work ... In You!

For God is working in you, giving you the desire to
obey Him and the power to do what pleases Him.
Philippians 2:13 NLT

Do you ever wonder what you can do for God?

You are important to God and your work is necessary to further His work. You're the hands, feet, voice and heart that He needs to get His job done. He is continually walking with you and He wants you to realize how much He needs you.

God wants to be near you and see you delight in the good things that come your way. He especially enjoys seeing you come to life when you're doing good deeds and thanking Him because you understand how loved you really are.

It's a new day. Give God a chance to work wonders in you!

A Taste of Goodness
Lord, thank You for all the good things You do in my life. Help me to return those favors cheerfully by helping those around me. Amen.

Starting Over

*For I can do everything with the help
of Christ who gives me the strength I need.*

Philippians 4:13 NLT

Each new day brings its ups and downs and it seems like we're always starting over in one way or another. We need to embrace each new day with a clean heart, a positive attitude and a willingness to serve.

Whatever you are planning, remember that Christ will give you the strength to move forward. Goethe said,

*Whatever you can do, or dream you can, begin it.
Boldness has genius, power and magic in it.
Only engage, and then the mind grows heated.
Begin it and the work will be completed.*

Begin the new day, the new job, the new life, and know that you are strengthened every step of the way by God's love.

A Taste of Peace

Lord, it isn't easy to feel totally at peace when starting something new. Remind me today that whatever I do, You'll be right there with me. Amen.

When It's Time To Quiet Down

"Be silent, and know that I am God! I will be honored by every nation. I will be honored throughout the world."
Psalm 46:10 NLT

Have you ever considered how much noise filters through your brain every day? From the moment you wake up until you close your eyes again at night, you have almost no quiet moments.

If you don't have quiet moments, it becomes harder and harder to think your own thoughts and almost impossible to hear the voice of your Savior. If the still small voice is trying to communicate with you, it may be drowned out by the noise outside or inside your mind. Take a minute, breathe deeply, shut out the world and invite your Father into your heart and mind.

Meister Eckhart said, "The very best and highest attainment in this life is to remain still and let God act and speak in you." Reach up. Reach out to God and let Him speak to you today.

A Taste of Faithfulness
Lord, it is so easy for me to ignore You in the midst of the turmoil around and in me all the time. Help me find peace in You today. Amen.

Making the Impossible Happen

Jesus told them, "I assure you, even if you had faith
as small as a mustard seed you could say to
this mountain, 'Move from here to there,' and
it would move. Nothing would be impossible."
Matthew 17:20 NLT

Many of us feel that we don't have enough faith. Part of the reason could be that we don't ask God to help us with all things, no matter how big or small. If we did, we'd come back and ask for help with even bigger things. It's quite interesting that we don't need huge faith for big things to happen. We just have to have faith.

Norman Vincent Peale said, "No matter how dark things seem to be or actually are, raise your sights and see possibilities – always see them, for they're always there."

It's a new day. Have the faith to make impossible things happen. How much bigger can you think today?

A Taste of Faithfulness
Lord, I have to admit that I don't always have enough faith. Help me to believe in the impossible. Help me to receive more of You. Amen.

The Perfect Day

When the clouds are heavy, the rains come down. When a tree falls, whether south or north, there it lies. If you wait for perfect conditions, you will never get anything done.

Ecclesiastes 11:3-4 NLT

Do you ever dissuade yourself from looking for a new job because you have to wait for the perfect conditions? Perhaps you tell yourself that once you've completed your current project, then you'll be able to start another one, even if the current one no longer serves your needs.

The person looking for the perfect mate might miss the perfect mate simply because they didn't know what to look for. When the conditions for change are ripe, change happens. Waiting for perfect opportunities and perfect partners may result in never getting the job done.

It's a new and perfect day to move forward. May the fruit of your spirit be one of joy and may you have a positive desire to let things happen.

A Taste of Joy

Lord, remind me that this is a perfect day for me to do what You have designed me to do. Amen.

Slightly Used Pots

*"And yet, LORD, You are our Father. We are the clay, and
You are the potter. We are all formed by Your hand."*

Isaiah 64:8 NLT

You might feel like a slightly used pot instead of a
brand new one at the moment. Perhaps the material
that makes you "you" isn't brand new. But you can
renew your heart, mind and attitude each day.

What do you see when you look in the mirror?
Once you get past the idea that you're growing older and you have to work harder than ever to stay in
shape, you need to keep looking. You need to see
the one the Lord loves and nurtures. You are being
molded and shaped and smoothed a bit more every
day by God's loving hands. You are becoming all
that He meant for you to be.

Look again. What do you see now? You should
be seeing one of the most beautiful creations on
earth, the unique person designed to do wonderful things for your Father in heaven. The Potter is
proud of you.

A Taste of Patience

Lord, I'm not always sure I'm special. Help me to see
myself as You see me now. Amen.

The Good You Can Do!

"Love your enemies, do good to them, and lend to them without expecting to get anything back. Then your reward will be great, and you will be [children] of the Most High."

Luke 6:35

Most of us enjoy doing good things for others. We especially like to do good things for the people we love and the friends that help make life more valuable. It seems like a natural thing for us to do.

This passage in Luke offers a whole different approach. It says that we need to love our enemies and be good to them. Let's think about that. First of all, you probably don't have any real enemies, but there are people in your life that you are distancing yourself from for some reason.

What should you do for them? What can you do to improve these relationships? Luke tells you to keep giving and keep lending and keep nurturing until you no longer have an enemy ... but a friend.

A Taste of Goodness

Lord, I know You said we should love our enemies, but I sometimes struggle to love them. Ignoring them was an easy way out. Help me find ways to be good to them for Your sake. Amen.

August

Walking the Walk

*In his heart a man plans his course,
but the LORD determines his steps.*
Proverbs 16:9

We often talk about "walking the walk" in Christian circles. The idea is that we need to walk in Jesus' shoes and live a life that exemplifies His love for others. We need to be better followers.

Sometimes we aren't even clear on where we need to "walk the walk." Are we only doing it when we attend a Bible study or go to church on Sundays? Could we be "walking the walk" when we offer to pray for someone when we don't know anything about their faith?

Take a look at your plans for today, and then look at them again tonight before you go to bed. Can you identify moments where God directed your steps? Can you see the places that He led you ... the places where you were really "walking the walk"?

Walk with Him today and see what wonderful surprises He has in store for you.

A Taste of Faithfulness
Lord, make me willing to walk wherever You would have me go. Amen.

Discovering the Difference

When you bow down before the Lord and admit your
dependence on Him, He will lift you up and give you honor.
James 4:10 NLT

Most of us know the Serenity Prayer. Reinhold
Niebhur directed our thoughts when he wrote,
"God, grant me the serenity to accept the things I
cannot change; the courage to change the things I
can, and the wisdom to know the difference."

Determining "the difference" between the things
we have to accept and those we need to change is
very important.

Acceptance also requires courage. Knowing "the
difference" involves wisdom. It is wise to put the
circumstances before the Lord and admit your dependence on Him.

The God of peace, courage and wisdom, will lift
you up and help you to determine the difference in
every situation you face. He will show you whether
you have to accept or change the situation.

A Taste of Peace

Lord, I seek Your peace in all situations where I struggle
to make a difference. Help me desire Your will in all
things. Amen.

The Winds of Change

May the LORD bless you and protect you.
May the LORD smile on you and be gracious to you.
May the LORD show you His favor and give you His peace.

Numbers 6:24 NLT

Do you notice all the things that need to be changed in the world?

If things bother you, the winds of change are stirring around you for a reason. They are blowing opportunities right into your path. You could do something about them. Change cannot happen on its own. It needs a constant force behind it. If you find that a certain passion is brewing within you to get something done, then God may well be appointing you to do it.

Changing things isn't easy, but if you're doing God's will doors will open to make those changes possible. God will bless you with His peace when you become His voice for change.

A Taste of Peace

Lord, help me know when I need to enforce change for good in my neighborhood and grant me Your peace. Amen.

Ripe for the Picking

*What does the Lord require of you? To act justly and
to love mercy and to walk humbly with your God.*
Micah 6:8

Sometimes choices resemble fruit on a tree. Easy decisions are like low-hanging fruit which is easy to pick. Difficult decisions require us to look a little higher for fruit that is ripe for the picking. How must we go about making these more difficult decisions?

The first step is to know what God wants from you. He's already blessed the fruit on your tree and the potential choices you might make. How do you decide which ones will help you become more of what He wants you to be? Will you reach high enough to walk more humbly with God and reach out in mercy and love toward others?

Look beyond the low hanging fruit and find the precious fruit above. You'll be glad you made the effort.

A Taste of Goodness

Lord, help me to choose the ripe fruit of love and mercy and help me share that with everyone I meet today. Amen.

Weeds of Worry

*Humble yourselves, therefore, under God's mighty
hand, that He may lift you up in due time. Cast all
your anxiety on Him because He cares for you.*

1 Peter 5:6-7

To worry is like having weeds in your garden. They seem to pop up everywhere and if there are too many, they choke the good and healthy plants.

Worries seem to come at us from every direction and if we uproot one, another comes and plants itself. We feel suffocated by life and wonder why we can't feel the sunshine.

You may not be able to keep worry from sprouting but you can decide what to do when it comes along. You can hand it over to the Master Gardener and allow Him to deal with it. Your job is simply to keep growing right where you are and to let God handle the rest. Before long, you may not even notice a stray worry that appears because the Gardener will take care of it.

Grow in His light and expect His blessings.

A Taste of Peace

Lord, worry steals my peace. Help me to weed it out of my life and hand it over to You as quickly as possible. Amen.

The Right Track

*Be strong and steady, always enthusiastic
about the Lord's work, for you know that
nothing you do for the Lord is ever useless.*
1 Corinthians 15:58 NLT

Will Rogers reminds us, "Even if you're on the right
track, you'll get run over if you just sit there."

It's always good to keep moving, growing, and
going in God's direction for you. It might be time to
build up steam and check with the Conductor to see
where He would like you to go.

If you're not on the right track, this is your invi-
tation to adjust your course. After all, the journey
isn't over and you still have time to move forward.
Everything you do for God on the trip counts and
He's proud of your work. If you want to do more
for Him, He'll bless you all of the way.

A Taste of Self-control

Lord, help me to desire to do the work You have planned
for me. Keep me running in the direction of the dreams
that are mine to complete for You. Amen.

Turnips and Peas

All a man's ways seem innocent to him,
but motives are weighed by the LORD.
Proverbs 16:2

God looks directly into our hearts and knows what makes us tick.

Motivation is about what makes us turn up for work to be done. In a garden, we might say there are always some turnips. They "turn up" for the hard work, or the fun work, or they don't "turn up" at all. It doesn't take too much digging to figure out who's going to be a turnip when things need to be done.

The peas are a little harder. We find the *p*rocrastinators, the *p*hilosophers and the picky *p*'s who just make the job hard on everyone. It's good to hoe around the *p*'s a bit and find the positive ones will want to just help.

Whether you feel more like the turnips or the peas, just remember God knows what work you did in the garden.

A Taste of Goodness

Lord, help me to be readily available when someone needs me. Remind me that You are always there for me and I need to do more to nurture Your garden. Amen.

Caught Unawares and Dumbfounded

*Give your burdens to the L*ORD*, and He will take care of you. He will not permit the godly to slip and fall.*
Psalm 55:22 NLT

Have you ever been caught totally unawares by something? Maybe you were suddenly fired from a job, or a relationship of several years suddenly ended. Whatever it was, it probably left you speechless, dumbfounded, totally amazed and shaken.

When that happens to us, we have to choose how to react. We can suffer in silence and develop ulcers, we can yell at the top of our lungs, or we can pray fervently for God's help and surrender all to Him. When it comes to personal sorrows, we have no choice but to pray.

You were not created to carry your burdens alone. You have to put them down at the foot of the Cross. Your Father knows what to do from there.

A Taste of Peace
Lord, when a crisis comes into my life, I'm anything but peaceful. Help me to give my burdens to You and wait for Your guidance. Amen.

Success and Failure

*"For I know the plans I have for you," says
the LORD. "They are plans for good and not for
disaster, to give you a future and a hope."*
Jeremiah 29:11 NLT

When you have set yourself goals, you have to realize that you do not always have control over the outcome. Sometimes you will succeed, but other times not. When your ideas are rejected you feel that you have failed.

If you didn't focus on your objective or make a solid effort, then it may be your fault. Otherwise it's simply a sign for you to try another route or reevaluate your goal. Sometimes rejection can actually steer you in the right direction.

Imagine being Edison trying for the 1999th time. Would you try one more time? If success has anything to do with attitude, persistence and faith, then your chances of being victorious are good. God wants you to succeed in the plans He has designed for you.

A Taste of Faithfulness
Lord, please give me the right perspective when things don't seem to be going my way. Let me see Your hand in all I do. Amen.

Ark Building

Be strong and courageous. Don't be afraid or discouraged.
1 Chronicles 22:13

Imagine yourself in Noah's position. You're on dry land without a cloud in the sky and no one has ever heard of rain. You believe that God has given you instructions to build a great big boat because the earth is going to be destroyed by water. Your neighbors are convinced that you've lost your mind. You are obedient to God, so you keep building.

You then gather every type of animal to enter the ark. Your friends are in hysterics now.

Even though you know how Noah's story ends, you don't know how your story will end. The question is not if you believe God, but if you believe God so implicitly that you'd build an ark in the middle of the city or town you live in, if He asked you to.

A Taste of Faithfulness
Lord, I try to follow Your rules and Your plans for my life. Help me to have Noah's faith, because I want to bravely follow wherever You lead. Amen.

Blushing Again!

Even fools are thought to be wise when they keep silent;
when they keep their mouths shut, they seem intelligent.

Proverbs 17:28 NLT

Have you ever felt embarrassed about something you've said? You made a comment that made you blush and you're not quite sure how to recover from it. To retreat seems the best option.

The truth is, most of the things that make you blush aren't really worth feeling embarrassed about. When you have said or done something embarrassing, you are bound to realize your mistake. You then have the opportunity to make amends and make sure it never happens again.

Let's not be embarrassed over insignificant things. Let's be embarrassed if we neglect important spiritual matters. Let's find a way to speak up for God or to keep quiet in obedience to God. Then all will be as it should be.

A Taste of Patience

Lord, I'm sometimes not patient enough to wait when I disagree with someone. Direct my thoughts and lead my actions according to Your will. Amen.

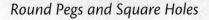

Round Pegs and Square Holes

This is the day that the LORD has made;
let us rejoice and be glad in it.
Psalm 118:24

Are you the same person today that you were yesterday, last week or a year ago? If you're growing, then you're constantly improving and becoming more mature. You may have discovered that the new you isn't compatible with your old life.

If you're becoming new in the Lord, you start to think in new ways. You grasp things you never understood before. You live differently. You become a round peg in a square hole and things simply have to change.

Today is a new day and you're on a path of discovery. Reach up and connect to the Source of light and love and let Him show you where you'll fit the best. Celebrate all that life brings you today and give God the glory!

A Taste of Goodness
Lord, I'm growing and changing and sometimes I'm afraid of what it implies. Help me to move in the direction that will bring us both great joy! Amen.

Bend, Don't Break!

I love the LORD, for He heard my voice;
He heard my cry for mercy. Because He turned His
ear to me, I will call on Him as long as I live.
Psalm 116:1-2

Some of us are not very flexible. We cannot bend very far without serious consequences. We're comfortable as we are and moving from our comfort zone makes us unhappy.

God wants you to reach a little further than you're used to today. Accept greater challenges to serve His people. Help carry someone's burden or just hug someone with a spirit of warmth and caring. It's good to do some flexibility exercises every day. You'll discover that you become more flexible if you make the effort. It's much more sensible to adapt and broaden your horizons than it is to break.

The Lord listens to your heart, softens it, and enables it to care for others.

A Taste of Peace
Lord, I am still so set in my ways. Help me to become more flexible so that I will be able to love and serve others as You would have me do. Amen.

Time is on Your Side

We know that God causes everything to
work together for the good of those who love God
and are called according to His purpose for them.

Romans 8:28 NLT

The concept of time is somewhat mind-boggling. It can crawl along, and almost comes to a standstill when you're waiting for something important.

Yet, when another birthday approaches you feel almost helpless at how quickly time passes. The years seem to be spinning out of control and you've reached the age your mother was when you thought she was old.

So, what are you planning today? How will you use the hours and minutes God has given you? How will you make the most of your time? You will have to trust that you are in the exact place that God wants you to be at this moment. Rejoice and be glad and do the work you've been called to do.

A Taste of Patience

Lord, help me to live every moment fully aware that I am doing everything for Your glory. Amen.

The Clouds are Gathering

Examine yourselves to see if your faith is really genuine. Test yourselves. If you cannot tell that Jesus Christ is among you, it means you have failed the test.
2 Corinthians 13:5 NLT

Each of us has to struggle through some dense clouds in our lives on earth. Read the Psalms and draw some comfort from the fact that the ancients felt the same way. Those times are part of our journey and help us grow more than we might ever realize.

God has a plan for your life and He won't let go of you. Keep praying and keep checking to see if He's near regardless of how you feel. You'll soon discover that He's been with you all along.

God is waiting ahead to help you and to heal you. He is there standing in the light and will shine it on you to direct your path.

A *Taste of Faithfulness*
Lord, please keep walking with me on my journey through life. I'm not always sure I can see which way to go. Lead me and shine Your light on my path. Amen.

Just Get Started!

So take a new grip with your tired hands and stand firm on your shaky legs. Mark out a straight path for your feet.
Hebrews 12:12-13 NLT

New developments bring a mixture of emotions that are both exciting and scary. You have to choose when a dream can come to life. Only you will know when you're ready to jump in and take a leap of faith. Remember that you are not alone because God walks with you every moment of your life.

He encourages you through His Spirit to act according to His will and purpose for you. He sends teachers, friends, and inspiration to keep you on the path. He also makes you aware of opportunities that will enable you to reach your goal.

It's your day to get started. Take that great idea or action that you've been holding on to for too long and give it wings. You'll be glad you did.

A Taste of Joy
Lord, there is great joy in getting started on a new adventure. Be with me as I try to stand firm in order to walk further down the path with You. Amen.

Why We Have Hope

We also rejoice in our sufferings, because we know that suffering produces perseverance; perseverance, character; and character, hope. And hope does not disappoint us, because God has poured out His love into our hearts by the Holy Spirit.

Romans 5:3-5

Doesn't it do your heart good to know that "God has poured out His love into our hearts by the Holy Spirit"?

That love is the reason why we have hope. Each time we face a trial and find our comfort in God's arms and our direction in His Word, then our hope rises. We know that we are never alone and that nothing can happen to us that He is not aware of.

When we keep going, trusting, and believing in what He has planned, then our character grows ever stronger and our hope stays alive. We have the hope that only the Heavenly Father bestows. Rejoice in sufferings and even more in your hope.

A Taste of Joy

Lord, we have walked a long way together and I have had my share of ups and downs. Thank You for always being with me, You are my everlasting hope. Amen.

Getting a Grasp on Faith

*Do not be discouraged, for the LORD
your God will be with you wherever you go.*

Joshua 1:9

Do you ever feel that you've bitten off more than you can chew?

Stop! Rest! Take time to listen to the Lord's quiet voice. He wants to make you aware of the things He wants you to do. He will help you to let go of the things that consume your time and energy unnecessarily.

Faith has a lot to do with letting go of anxiety and trusting in God's grace, mercy and guidance. If every day has two handles, you must decide to either grasp it with the handle of faith, or the handle of anxiety. Only one of those will hold you up and keep you strong.

Don't be discouraged, God is with you.

A Taste of Self-control
Lord, help me to face everything I do today with courage and great faith. Amen.

When Reason isn't Reasonable

"Come now, let us reason together," says the LORD.
Isaiah 1:18

We sometimes find it difficult to make sense of life. We try to understand perplexing things so that we can go on. We are good at it for the most part, but sometimes we find ourselves up against a wall without understanding what happened.

John Donne said, "Reason is our soul's left hand, Faith her right." Assuming that your stronger hand is your dominant right hand, that makes sense. Faith is the brother ally, reason the weaker cousin.

There are times when you cannot come up with easy answers for certain events that take place in your life or in the world. None of us will ever understand the great tragedies of hurricanes and earthquakes that claim human lives.

We can go to the Lord in faith and ask His help in discerning reasons. It's the reasonable thing to do.

A Taste of Reason
Lord, there are always more questions than answers when strange events happen in the world. Sometimes that's true of my life as well. Be with me today beyond reason, holding me up in faith. Amen.

Stepping Stones

*You have made a wide path
for my feet to keep them from slipping.*
2 Samuel 22:37 NLT

Do you remember skimming stones as a kid? Finding suitable stones to reach and stand on while trying to cross a stream without falling into the water was also a lot of fun. Sometimes those stones were slimy which made the balancing act a bit harder.

As an adult, it can seem like you're always trying to find the stones that are safe to stand on for a moment while you figure out your next move. Even now, some of those stepping stones are slippery and you only realize that when you stand on them.

Today remember that God doesn't want you to slip and fall beyond His grasp. He will hold you firmly and enable you to get safely to the place He wants you to go. You can even have fun while getting there.

A *Taste of Patience*
Sometimes Lord, I try to step out ahead of You under the impression that I can just skip across the water like a stone that won't sink. Help me to take each step with You and stand firmly in Your care. Amen.

The Wings of Faith

Those who wait on the LORD will find new strength.
They will fly high on wings like eagles. They will run
and not grow weary. They will walk and not faint.
Isaiah 40:31 NLT

Imagine flying up high in the sky and looking down at the world as you know it. Your perspective on things would change significantly. When you see the entire picture, you understand things in a new way. That's the perspective that God has on things. He sees the whole picture. He knows why it's important for you to go through what you're going through and that it will strengthen you and help your soul grow stronger.

Faith can enable us to fly high enough to get a new view. We have to desire to know God's vision for our lives and ask for His help in moving forward. Your wings are not clipped by adversity, they're strengthened. Get out there and fly higher!

A Taste of Faithfulness

Lord, I embrace the wings of hope and faith that You have given me. Help me to always try to understand Your intention for my life and spirit. Amen.

The Counselor Is Available

"If you love Me, obey My commandments.
And I will ask the Father, and He will give you
another Counselor, who will never leave you.
He is the Holy Spirit, who leads us into all truth."
John 14:15-17 NLT

God has appointed a Counselor who will never leave us – the Holy Spirit. His desire is for our well-being and to help us understand the Truth.

Truth is tricky. There is the Truth that applies to God, His Son Jesus and the Holy Spirit. But then, there are truths that we know about ourselves, our work or our interactions with others. There are even truths for us in certain situations that might not be truths for someone else in the same situation. Sometimes truth is very personal and that's why the Holy Spirit guides us fully into the truth about God and about ourselves.

The Counselor is available today and He's always willing to give guidance to those who love Him.

A Taste of the Spirit

Lord, guide me today in the truth that Your Holy Spirit would have me understand for my life at this stage. Amen.

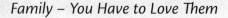

Family – You Have to Love Them

*Carry each other's burdens, and in this way
you will fulfill the law of Christ.*
Galatians 6:2

If you're lucky, you've got the perfect family. You love each other all the time, respect each other's boundaries, and agree with each other's goals. Wait a second, that's not luck, that's a fantasy. There isn't a family quite like that anywhere.

Even so, your family is your main support system. They are the ones who mold and shape you and inspire you to become more. As John Donne once wrote, "No man is an island." We're all part of other people's lives for a reason and we weren't meant to go it alone in the world.

Your family is your root, your support, and your blessing. Thank God for each person in your family today.

A Taste of Goodness
Lord, my family is important to me and I know they are important to You. Please help us to carry each other's burdens and enjoy each other's blessings. Amen.

Are You My Mother, My Sister, My Brother?

Whenever we have the opportunity, we should do good to everyone, especially to our Christian brothers and sisters.
Galatians 6:10 NLT

As you live, work and play among neighbors and friends, many of them become like your family. A new family might develop from a church group or a group with common cause.

Why do they become family? Because they are there to provide the essential ingredients of support, kindness and interest in your welfare. They become teachers, mentors and sponsors. They become sounding boards, helpers and volunteers to get you through the ups and downs of daily living.

As a member of this extended family, you learn to serve others in joy. You thank God for placing you in an extended family so you can understand how much He loves you. Your family is everywhere. Be sure to let them know how much you love them.

A Taste of Goodness
Lord, You are so good to me. Thank You for blessing me with a multitude of wonderful brothers and sisters. Amen.

Try a Little Kindness

Let us not become weary in doing good, for at the proper time we will reap a harvest if we do not give up. Therefore, as we have opportunity, let us do good to all people, especially to those who belong to the family of believers.

Galatians 6:9-10

We are each on a journey following where the Lord leads us. We're His voice and His hands in the world. William Penn wisely said, "If there be any kindness I can show, or any good thing I can do to any fellow being, let me do it now, and not deter or neglect it, as I shall not pass this way again."

When you meet people on your path, you might smile, offer a word of solace, give a gift, or lend a hand, and it will enrich their well-being as well as yours. Your kindness will make a difference in their lives and it will show God your heart.

Kindness opens doors, embraces weaker souls, and encourages downhearted spirits. Think of how often someone's kindness has made a difference in your life. Never grow weary of being kind.

A Taste of Kindness

Lord, bless those I meet today and remind me to offer a little kindness wherever I can. Help me to share Your light. Amen.

Embracing Forgiveness

The LORD is like a father to His children, tender and compassionate to those who fear Him. For He understands how weak we are; He knows we are only dust.

Psalm 103:13-14 NLT

Martin Luther King, Jr. said, "Forgiveness is not an occasional act: it is an attitude."

An attitude of forgiveness must be embraced, tutored, created, and shaped in you just like any other attitude or opinion you hold. The first person you must be willing to forgive is yourself. You must let go of those things you're not proud of so that you are not held back by those things.

What kind of action do you need to take? You need to embrace God's gift of forgiveness and then surrender all the acts that require forgiveness to Him. Once you've let go of those acts, leave them there and let Him help you become more of who He meant you to be.

You have the privilege to be loved and to be forgiven.

A Taste of Forgiveness

Lord, help me to be more forgiving to myself and to others in my life. Amen.

Be the First Forgiver

Then Peter came to Jesus and asked, "Lord, how many times shall I forgive my brother when he sins against me? Up to seven times?" Jesus answered, "I tell you, not seven times, but seventy-seven times."
Matthew 18:21-22 CEV

We live in a competitive world, which means that most of us are always concerned about being number one.

However, when it comes to forgiveness we're often more willing to wait it out and see if the other person offers forgiveness first. We can see where they were wrong, but we can't see where we were wrong.

When Peter asked Jesus about forgiveness, he may not have liked the answer. Peter was prepared to give someone a break at least seven times. Some of us would say that it was pretty generous. Discovering that he had to be that generous at least 490 times was a different thing.

Look at yourself today, think about those that need you to extend the hand of forgiveness. Go ahead, be first.

A Taste of Forgiveness
Lord, help me to forgive others as You forgive me every day. Amen.

It Only Takes a Spark

For God loves the person who gives cheerfully.
2 Corinthians 9:7 NLT

Most of us understand the concept that "little things can mean a lot." When you're on a sports field playing a tough match, it is most exciting if your team has that extra spark, the winning edge.

When you share your sandwich with a child who is hungry, it means a lot to see a smile light up a little face. When you give a little to help the needy, your efforts combined with every one else's efforts brings much joy.

The point is that we often miss doing the little things because we don't realize how important they are. Your small gift, whether it's a smile or a sandwich, is the spark that makes a difference. Your spark can light up the world.

Today find a way to make a difference. Be the spark that brightens someone else's life. Carry the torch of God's love for others and pass it along wherever you are.

A Taste of Love
Lord, help me to share Your love with others today and make a difference in any way that I can. Amen.

Gifts of the Heart

*"Do for others as you would
like them to do for you."*
Luke 6:31 NLT

Have you had the experience of diving in to promote a cause or help a friend and then celebrating the feeling of having accomplished much as a team? While celebrating, you perhaps even thought about your contribution and it made you feel even better.

Giving makes you feel good because you know that without the gift you contributed, the job might not have been done, or at least not as quickly. Giving makes living more joyful.

Today, look at the ways you give in thought, word, and deed. Thank God for giving you His love and a heart that wants to see the good in others.

A Taste of Goodness

Lord, You have given so much to me. Thank You for any opportunity I may have to give to others in Your name. Amen.

The "Got-to-Have" Frenzy

"You should remember the words of the Lord Jesus:
'It is more blessed to give than to receive.'"
Acts 20:35 NLT

Somewhere along the way while growing up, we got the impression that the person with the most material possessions wins. Ever since, we've been in a "got-to-have" frenzy.

Winston Churchill said, "We make a living by what we get. We make a life by what we give."

It's time for most of us to think more about giving, than getting. Keep in mind that even if you don't have all the latest gadgets on the market, if you have a bed at night, dinner on the table and have clean water to drink, you're living in a state of wealth.

Let's be grateful for all that we have today and thank God for His mercy in our lives. Then, let us be spurred on to give more to those in need.

A Taste of Giving
Lord, I praise You for providing all that I need in my life. Holy Spirit, lead me to share what I have with others. Amen.

Friendship Giving

*There is a time for everything,
a season for every activity under heaven.*
Ecclesiastes 3:1 NLT

*"Sometimes being a friend is mastering the art of timing.
There is time for silence. A time to let go and allow people
to hurl themselves into their own destiny. And a time to
prepare to pick up the pieces when it's all over."*

~ Octavia Butler

Friendship requires an interesting set of skills to make it work. You have to know when to jump in with advice and good intentions and when to back off and let your friend figure out things alone. You have to know when they need a laugh or a hug. Sometimes friends can share each other's burdens and sometimes friends can step back in when they're needed a bit later on.

As you think about your close friends today, honor them before God, and give Him praise for the many joys you share.

A Taste of Giving

Lord, my friend is so important to me and I'm not always sure how to best take care of her needs. Help me to be as giving and tender as possible today. Amen.

September

Follow Jesus

"You are My friends if you obey Me."
John 15:14 NLT

Remember when you were a kid you played a game called, "Follow the Leader"? You were supposed to imitate the leader's movements and actions, and try to keep up with the moves. The point of the game was not to think for yourself.

In your adult life, you may feel like that happens to you all the time. Your boss gives you an assignment and you do it without question. Your spouse wants you to go somewhere and you go. You're always following.

Jesus wants to know that you're following Him because you love Him and not because all the other people in your life are pulling you in His direction. Check your heart and get a clear understanding of what motivates you.

It's great to walk beside others in your life, but it's important to follow the leader, Jesus Christ.

A *Taste of Faithfulness*
Lord, help me follow in Your footsteps today so that every action I take receives Your blessing. Amen.

The Dimmer Switch

*A friend is always loyal, and a brother
is born to help in time of need.*
Proverbs 17:17 NLT

The friends in our lives are essential to our well-being. None of us would survive the journey if we had to walk it alone. It's all about the lessons learned, the memories created and the opportunities offered.

In any friendship, the roles constantly change. One offers strength in time of need, one finds a way to lighten up a situation, or one is just there to hold a hand. A true friend walks beside you whenever you need them. Friendship turns the light on, up or out, depending on the situation. Friendship is like a dimmer switch and when it's plugged into the Source of Light, it makes an amazing difference.

Today, celebrate your friends. Enjoy the delightful fact that God loves you so much, He provided friends to show you His love each day.

A Taste of Love
Lord, thank You for blessing me with friends who strengthen me, laugh with me, and make life worthwhile. Amen.

It's All Possible!

"Anything is possible for someone who has faith!"
Mark 9:23 CEV

Brother Lawrence said, "All things are possible to him who believes, yet more to him who hopes, more still to him who loves, and most of all to him who practices and perseveres in these three virtues."

Hope and love will get you on the right path and practice and perseverance will see that you get there. All things are possible but sometimes you have to be the catalyst to make things happen. You have to find the way through the obstacles, or have faith through the trials, or continue even when you've failed. You have to believe that the goal you've set is possible to achieve.

Believing it yourself may seem easy until your goal has not been reached within the set time limit. You might find yourself waiting, working and believing a lot longer than you expected. It's up to you to stay focused and faithful to your dreams.

A Taste of Patience

Lord, please help me to patiently hope and believe that my dreams are yet to be realized. Amen.

Purposeful Living

*For everything, absolutely everything, above
and below, visible and invisible ... everything got
started in Him and finds its purpose in Him.*
Colossians 1:16 THE MESSAGE

Sometimes we're reluctant to include God in our work or our special dreams. We may feel that those things are not as important to Him as our spiritual well-being. The truth is that you were designed with a specific purpose and God knows what you need to achieve it. As a Creator, He fully understands the joy when seeing an idea come to light or accomplishing something new. He applauds you when you are determined to achieve your life's purpose.

Today, you can turn all of your intentions over to Him. Ask Him to walk with you and help you create those dreams according to His will and purpose for your life. God can make anything happen.

A *Taste of Self-control*

Lord, I know that I need to step back from my dreams and invite You to come into them and help me achieve them. I give all my dreams to You and ask You to guide me. Amen.

You Are so Wonderfully Made!

*I praise You because of the wonderful way You created me.
Everything You do is marvellous! Of this I have no doubt ...
You saw my body being formed. Even before I was born, you
had written in your book everything I would do.*

Psalm 139:14-16 CEV

Isn't it awesome that you are so well-known? God created every fibre of your being. Every thought, every joy and experience life brings is in His care.

Charles H. Spurgeon said, "He who counts the stars and calls them by their names, is in no danger of forgetting His own children. He knows your case as thoroughly as if you were the only creature He ever made, or the only saint He ever loved."

As you consider your day today, reflect on what it means to be so fully known and loved. Consider and know that you are perfect in God's sight.

Your Creator created you for His glory in an awesome and unique way.

A Taste of Goodness

Lord, thank You for loving me so much and for blessing my life in so many ways. Give me joy in knowing You more fully today. Amen.

All God's Children

He came into His own world, but His own nation did not welcome Him. Yet some people accepted Him. So He gave them the right to be the children of God.

John 1:11-12 CEV

Do you remember your childhood? Do you remember the things that made you feel happy and excited and that gave you a sense of security and safety? Do you remember how loved you felt in your home, surrounded by people who nurtured you and cared for you every day and at every moment?

If you can remember those things or some part of them, then you have a tiny glimpse of what it means to be a child of God. Your Father in heaven, His Son and the Holy Spirit loves you. You are continually and always loved and protected and cared for. This idea should make you feel giddy. What an amazing thing it truly is!

Take some time today to let this truth sink in. Let the idea of being God's child give you pure joy. Thank Him for being such a wonderful Father.

A Taste of Love

Lord, I do thank You for loving me so much and for providing so well for my life. Amen.

Do You Really Want It Your Way?

And this world is fading away, along with everything it craves. But if you do the will of God, you will live forever.
1 John 2:17 NLT

Many of us have grown up in a world where we quickly learned that life is a competitive sport and we would either have to learn to play or sit on the sideline. In the struggle to come out on top, we are often determined that things should happen the way we want them to happen or not at all.

Every day we make a choice. We give God a passing nod on our way to work and say, "I'll check in with You at the end of the day or later in the week after the work is done." Or, we give the work to God and say, "Be with me and guide and direct my efforts according to Your will and purpose."

A Taste of Self-control

Lord, I am always trying to stay on top of things and take care of everything I'm responsible for. Please take all the things on my "To Do" list and help me understand which ones You most want me to do. Amen.

One Day at a Time

"So don't worry about tomorrow, for tomorrow will bring its own worries. Today's trouble is enough for today."
Matthew 6:34 NLT

If you were trying to convince me that you're not a worrier, I'd probably have trouble believing you since few of us are free of worry.

Most of the things we run through the worry mill never happen. Worry can keep you up half the night or simply ruin your day. Mary C. Crowley put it in context for us when she said, "Every evening I turn my worries over to God. He's going to be up all night anyway."

Maybe we need to learn to turn our worries over to God, knowing that He cares about us and wants to help us live more fully. Take it one day at a time. God will take care of everything for you.

A Taste of Self-control

Lord, I know that worry is a thing I can control if I just turn my troubles over to You. Help me believe that You will take care of even the small details of my life. Amen.

Believe It or Not!

How great is our Lord! His power is absolute!
His understanding is beyond comprehension!
Psalm 147:5 NLT

We try to understand our Supreme Creator in a way that helps us digest His will and strive to live according to His purpose. Wherever the quest leads is important because God Himself is leading us there.

Miguel de Unamuno tried to distinguish between a belief in the idea of God and a true belief in God Himself. He said, "Those who believe that they believe in God, but without passion in their hearts, without anguish in mind, without uncertainty, without doubt, without an element of despair even in their consolation, believe in the God idea, not God Himself."

In other words, your faith in God becomes more real as your passion for Him becomes more real. Believe it or not, your faith will strengthen you and answer your questions.

A Taste of Faithfulness
Lord, help me to trust You for Your guidance in every area of my life. Amen.

Hey, Why Are You Hiding?

*Toward evening they heard the L*ORD *God walking*
about in the garden, so they hid themselves among the trees.
*The L*ORD *God called to Adam, "Where are you?"*

Genesis 3:8-9 NLT

When we think or do something that we don't want
to share with the Lord, we try to find a place to hide.
We might think that because we're not in church or
addressing God in prayer, that He is not paying attention to what we're doing. Just like Adam and
Eve though, He knows exactly where we are all the
time. We can't ever hide from Him.

Once we understand this, it's a little easier to realize that we may as well come clean with God and
let Him know that we have done wrong and that
we'd appreciate His help. We're not looking for a
carte blanche so that we can do anything we want.
We're looking for ways to invite Him into our lives
and come out of hiding. He's waiting for you today.

A Taste of Self-control

Lord, I ask You to be with me in all that I do today and
help me to make wise and loving choices according to
Your will and purpose. Amen.

The Home Planet

But God made the earth by His power, and He
preserves it by His wisdom. He has stretched
out the heavens by His understanding.
Jeremiah 10:12 NLT

Earth is your home. Every day and every night, it sustains you and nourishes you and provides for you. Whether you live in the city or the country, by oceans or in the deserts, you are a guest here. You are here at God's bidding and by His design and this home is not to be taken for granted.

Rebecca Harding Davis wrote, "We are all of us from birth to death guests at a table which we did not spread. The sun, the earth, love, friends, our very breath are parts of the banquet ... Shall we think of the day as a chance to come nearer to our Host, and to find out something of Him who has fed us for so long?"

As you embrace the new day, thank God for providing such bounty for you.

A Taste of Goodness

Lord, You have provided so richly for me and I sometimes forget to thank You for Your goodness. I praise and thank You, Divine Creator, for knowing me so well. Amen.

Abundant Living

Always be full of joy in the Lord. I say it again – rejoice!
Let everyone see that you are considerate in all you do.
Philippians 4:4-5 NLT

Have you ever stopped to think about what you are thinking? Most of us have minds that store so many unnecessary negative thoughts that it has become imperative for us to launch a clean-up operation. We need to rid our systems of grime on a daily basis.

When your thoughts are happy and positive and full of grace, you're a different person. You're more productive, more fun to be around and you provide for the needs of others without even thinking.

Learn to think better thoughts and you might learn to create better actions. The universe started as a thought, then God spoke it into existence. Your thoughts and your actions are powerful. Let joy be one of the best thoughts and responses to God today.

A Taste of Joy

Lord, I don't thank You enough for the joys in my life.
I will think about them today and praise Your name.
Amen.

A Matter of Grace

May the Lord be with your spirit. Grace be with you all.
2 Timothy 4:22 NLT

Living in God's grace is a comforting thought. It's amazing to know that somehow we can make mistakes and receive forgiveness. God continues to bear with us, allowing us to learn and grow and become what He would like us to be. We appreciate the good things that sustain us and we marvel at being saved from those things that might do us harm. This is how we live under His grace, every day.

That we don't deserve grace is a given. If we got what we truly deserved from God, we'd most likely not survive. Today, it would be good to not only rejoice in the grace that you receive, but to think about the grace that you extend to others.

Are you willing to give others the grace that God so lovingly gives to you? As you walk in His grace today, look for opportunities to extend His grace to those around you. You will know that the Lord is with your spirit as you do so.

A Taste of Kindness

Lord, I am grateful that Your grace sustains me. Help me to share the gift of grace with those around me today. Amen.

The Road Not Taken

*"Be strong and courageous. Do not be terrified;
do not be discouraged, for the LORD your
God will be with you wherever you go."*

Joshua 1:9

Robert Frost's famous poem *The Road Not Taken*, is about two paths. One path is well worn and the other isn't well mapped out. Frost finally decides to take the road "less traveled by."

We're constantly faced with divergent paths and we have to take the risk of determining which way to go. The safe route is always tempting because we know that not much will be expected of us. The uncertain route is much more difficult. It may prove not to be worth the risk, or it may offer more than we ever hoped for.

Life keeps asking you to make choices. If you're strong and courageous, you could be off on a great new adventure. What will you choose today?

A Taste of Goodness

Lord, thank You for giving me wonderful opportunities and for being with me in the choices I make. Help me to be willing to step out in faith to take the road less traveled. Amen.

On Overload?

*The LORD is faithful in all He says; He is gracious
in all He does. The LORD helps the fallen
and lifts up those bent beneath their loads.*

Psalm 145:13-14 NLT

Do you have days when you feel that your circuits
are simply overloaded?

We have to complete a quota at work, manage a
household and somehow find time to breathe and
pray. We try to find some time to exercise, be social,
be a volunteer and go to church. Before we know it,
it has become more than we can handle.

The Creator who wanted us to live in the Garden
of Eden didn't have this scenario in mind. He desired a fulfilling life for us. A life of peace and harmony in which we look for ways to care for Him
and others.

Take some time today and get back to the garden. Bask in the coolness of the shade God provides
and enjoy His peace. Rest in God's care.

A Taste of Peace

Lord, I am constantly on the run and I would welcome
some time to simply relax with You today. Help me to
return to the garden of Your grace and glory. Amen.

The Best You and the Worst You

If part of a batch of dough is made holy by being offered to God, then all the dough is holy. If the roots of a tree are holy, the rest of the tree is holy too.
Romans 11:16 CEV

The Scripture from Romans is a great reminder that even though we may not be perfect, if we offer a part of ourselves to God, we offer our whole selves to Him. The individual parts that we haven't turned over to Him are perhaps those He is still helping us channel in the right direction so to live more in keeping with His intention for us.

As you consider where you are in life, your successes and your defeats, your good qualities and those you'd rather sweep under the rug, know that you are never out of reach of God's mercy and grace. He sees you as holy whenever He sees His Son in you. Let the Spirit guide your life into God's grace and bring you joy.

A Taste of Faithfulness
Lord, thank You for creating a way for me to constantly share Your grace and mercy. Amen.

In a Rut

If you are wise and understand God's ways, live a life of steady goodness so that only good deeds will pour forth.
James 3:13 NLT

Sometimes we feel as if we're stuck in a rut.

You needn't continue experiencing this feeling. Look for small things to free you from feeling stuck. Doing good for others is one such thing.

Broaden your horizons by volunteering in an area that is different from anything you have done. Learn a new skill or start a new hobby. It will stimulate your creativity and may give you new ideas.

Doing good deeds will also remind you that there are many people in the world who may not be as privileged as you, but still manage to smile and be positive.

A Taste of Goodness

Lord, I don't always know how to help others because I have so much trouble escaping from my own thoughts. Help me to find more positive ways to live and share the bounty You have given me. Amen.

Us vs. Them

*Yet we hear that some of you are living idle lives,
refusing to work and wasting time meddling in other
people's business. In the name of the Lord Jesus Christ,
we appeal to such people – no, we command them:
Settle down and get to work. Earn your own living.*

2 Thessalonians 3:11-12 NLT

We may be better at pointing out other people's faults and weaknesses than we are at seeing our own. We can easily adopt an "us-versus-them" mentality where we point out that "they" just don't get it and "we" have to figure it out for them.

When you start focusing on "them" and start wondering why they don't live up to your standards, it's time to remember that meddling in other people's business, never did serve them well. However casually you may judge others, stop now and get on with your own life.

A Taste of Patience
Lord, I know I'm not always patient with those around me and I expect them to take care of life the same way I would. Help me to see them and love them as You do and stop trying to be the judge. Amen.

Bless the Loaves and Fishes!

He took the five loaves and two fish, looked up toward heaven, and asked God's blessing on the food.
Matthew 14:19 NLT

Some families say grace before every meal. Some say grace just at dinner and some don't ever say grace. Which ever way you practiced it in your home, you may not have given much thought as to why you actually did it.

Jesus offered a blessing or a prayer of thanks before every meal. He showed us that we should thank God for providing the food that we eat and the basic necessities of life. When Jesus blessed the bread, there seemed to be more of it to share. With five loaves and two fish multitudes were fed and some was left over.

Before you consume one bite of the Chicken Kiev or the grilled salmon, bow your head to the Giver of all life and all nourishment and thank Him first.

A Taste of Faithfulness

Lord, bless the food that I am blessed to share with those around me today. Thank You for taking such good care of my basic needs. Amen.

Head and Shoulders above the Rest

Grow in the special favor and knowledge
of our Lord and Savior Jesus Christ.
2 Peter 3:18 NLT

We grow in knowledge by what we take in, but we grow in our capacity to give and love by what we give. We're designed to grow and God created all things so that we could do just that.

You can have excellent intellectual knowledge of the Bible for instance. You can know every Scripture and just when to quote it, but still be ignorant about God's Word. Your ignorance doesn't have anything to do with what you know, it's about what you do with what you know. God speaks to the heart and searches the motives of the heart. He cares about why you do something.

It's another day for you to shine and since you have faith in Jesus, you're already head and shoulders above the rest. See what you can do to grow in the special favor of the Lord today.

A Taste of Self-control

Lord, I have been reading Your Word but I'm not always good at giving from the heart. Help me to implement the knowledge I have in a practical way. Amen.

No Longer a Child

When I was a child, I talked like a child,
I thought like a child, I reasoned like a child.
When I became a man, I put childish ways behind me.

1 Corinthians 13:11

Can you remember your dreams, the fun stuff, and the way you thought about life as a child? By now you've learned that a lot of those things were viewed from a childlike perspective that must be put aside when a more adult perspective is needed.

It's okay to grow up. In fact, it's natural. Growing and changing are all aspects of the journey we're on to become more like Christ.

Augustine of Hippo said, "If you are pleased with what you are, you have stopped already. If you say, 'It is enough,' you are lost. Keep on walking, moving forward, trying for the goal. Don't try to stop on the way, or to go back, or to deviate from it."

Let the Holy Spirit lead you and cause you to grow in faith.

A Taste of Self-control

Lord, I am not always willing to keep growing, I even hope to stay put. Help me to keep going to the place You would have me go now. Amen.

Broken Pottery

And yet, LORD, You are our Father. We are the clay, and You are the potter. We are all formed by Your hand.

Isaiah 64:8 NLT

If you've ever created objects with clay, you know that it is both versatile and fragile. Sometimes you create beautiful objects and other times you simply pound the clay back down and start again.

Sometimes we're just a lump of clay, without shape, movement, or special beauty. We only start on the right track when we ask God to shape us.

In the process of being carefully molded a lot of things can happen. Sometimes we have setbacks and can feel utterly broken. Other times, we're functioning at a high level and are strengthened by the Potter's Hand. Whether you feel broken or whole or misshapen or beautiful, remember that you are always being lovingly formed by the Master.

A Taste of Peace
Lord, I get pretty frustrated when I feel that I've missed the mark and fallen down in the process of getting Your work done. Shape me with Your loving hand today. Amen.

The Reality of Hope

*What is faith? It is the confident assurance
that what we hope for is going to happen. It is
the evidence of things we cannot yet see.*
Hebrews 11:1 NLT

When we were children, we hoped for a new bike or a puppy. We hoped because we hadn't yet experienced the power of prayer and we believed somehow that to hope would bring the desired result.

Actually, we were on the right track back then. Hope often brings the desired result because we couple hope with the faith we have in Jesus Christ. The Hope of the Ages is with us still, every day, watching over us and challenging us to be faithful.

As you walk through your day today, think for a moment about the things that you hoped for yesterday and acknowledge the things you hope for today. Then pray about those things and feel confidently assured that God is at work in your life.

A Taste of Hope

Father, there are many times that I think I'll simply lose hope and then You powerfully remind me that You are always with me. Thank You for Your love. Amen.

What You See is What You Get!

We know that in all things God works
for the good of those who love Him, who
have been called according to His purpose.
Romans 8:28

You need to entrust your vision to God and walk with Him toward the goal. If you know where you want to go, it's a lot easier to get there when you focus on your vision of hope. What you see even in your imagination, is really what you can achieve. Seeing is believing!

When you become disillusioned, the disappointments of life can make it hard for you to stay focused and to keep surrendering your goal to God. The clouds of doubt will disappear as your hope grows and your faith becomes stronger.

Today you're encouraged to hold on to your dreams. God will bring everything together for your good at the right time. Trust that He has a plan for your life.

A Taste of Faithfulness
Lord, help me to continue in my hope and my faith in You to accomplish all the things that are mine to do. Thank You for Your endless blessings! Amen.

Guarding Your Heart

Above all else, guard your heart,
for it affects everything you do.
Proverbs 4:23 NLT

Protecting your heart is a serious matter especially if your heart has been broken before.

Many things other than romance can cause you heartache. You might experience the death of a friend, the anger of a child, the loss of a job that you really enjoyed, or not achieving a goal. You will come across many things in your life that can damage your heart in a number of ways. The best you can do is try to protect yourself.

You also need to pray for God's protection. Ask Him to be with you when you feel uncertain about a situation, to strengthen and renew you and help you to move on. Stay totally connected to the One who wants your heart to be blessed always.

A Taste of Self-control

Lord, I have trouble protecting my heart. I pray that You will renew my spirit and keep me safe in Your presence. Amen.

Speaking from the Heart

"For out of the overflow of the heart the mouth speaks."
Matthew 12:34

Speaking from the heart is not the same as just talking. When you do feel passionate about a topic it's a whole different conversation. You're involved and listening attentively, your body is poised because you don't want to miss a word.

In much the same way you can speak passionately about compassion. When you speak from the heart with kindness and love toward those around you, you make a positive impression on your listeners and bless them with your words. Speaking from the heart is about you sharing the deeper intentions of your heart and mind with others.

Today, listen to what your heart has to say.

A Taste of Goodness

Lord, I am grateful that You have blessed me with a loving heart. Grant that I might find ways to share my joy with others today. Amen.

Creating the Right Heart

"You must love the Lord your God with all your heart, all your soul, all your mind, and all your strength."
Mark 12:30 NLT

The world can be a confusing place and sometimes we feel uncertain about the future or how to handle change.

Confucius said, "To put the world in order, we must first put the nation in order; to put the nation in order, we must put the family in order; to put the family in order, we must cultivate our personal life; and to cultivate our personal life, we must first set our hearts right."

We're in the process of setting our hearts right. Jesus said that we should seek God with all of our heart, mind and soul.

Today is a great day to do some housecleaning. Give yourself a chance to sweep out cobwebs of doubt and worry, and ask God to help you create a more loving heart so that you can help improve the future by creating a more fruitful present.

A Taste of Love

Lord, create a clean heart in me today and renew a right spirit within me so that I can love You more. Amen.

Don't Lose Heart!

*"Look! Here I stand at the door and knock.
If you hear Me calling and open the door, I will
come in, and we will share a meal as friends."*

Revelation 3:20 NLT

There are times when we simply lose heart because of the things going on around us. We don't care as much about others, we can't really hear God no matter how loudly He may be knocking at our door. We're simply not able to serve the needs of anyone, especially ourselves.

If your heart needs repairing, ask God to heal it and move on. There are a lot of good things that you need to know and a lot of good people waiting to connect with you.

Even more important is the Spirit of your Heavenly Father who is waiting to remind you that He is always available. He will help you in any way so that you can continue joyfully. Don't lose heart, the Lord is there for you.

A Taste of Faithfulness
Lord, help me to lean on You today. My heart needs Your rejuvenating power. Amen.

Follow Your Heart

For the LORD sees every heart and understands and knows every plan and thought. If you seek Him, you will find Him.
1 Chronicles 28:9 NLT

People often advise you to follow your heart, but it's not that easy.

How do you follow your heart when it's tied to someone else's heart or in conflict with someone else's goals? Let's say you get a great job in another city, but your grown-up children are not happy because you'll have to move and they like having you nearby. Ultimately, you have to follow your heart and go where you feel you need to be so that your own goals can be accomplished.

Not even the wisest of us have all the answers. Ask God to lead you on the path He has planned for your life. Then to follow your heart will be easy.

A Taste of Self-control
Lord, it isn't always easy to figure out the next steps or the wisest course of action. Help me to follow You and create each step according to Your wisdom. Amen.

The Heart of Honesty

"As for you, if you walk before Me in integrity of heart and uprightness ... and do all I command, I will establish your royal throne over Israel forever."

1 Kings 9:4-5

Whatever happened to integrity? Do you remember when you were growing up and your mom insisted that you had to tell the truth even when you knew you were going to get into trouble. Well, you told the truth anyway.

Somewhere along the way, a lot of people have forgotten the values they were raised with. They've forgotten that it's still important to tell the truth and to be honest with others. In a world that is learning not to trust and uphold the values it was intended to have, you're being asked to look at yourself and decide if you present truth squarely and fairly each day.

Honesty is a virtue you need to nurture. You'll be glad when you do ... honest!

A Taste of Honesty

Lord, let the sweet fruit of honesty come from my heart and my lips in all my actions and interactions with others and especially with You. Amen.

October

Set the Bar a Little Higher

*"What good is it for a man to gain
the whole world, yet forfeit his soul?"*
Mark 8:36

If you watch an athlete do a pole vault or a high jump, you'll notice that after every jump, they set the bar a little higher before jumping again. Each time they reach for a higher goal.

It's good to see where we've set the bar for our own goals and standards. How hard do we work to achieve our expectations?

We must always strive to set the bar higher on things like our prayer time, our Bible reading, our relationships and our time with our loved ones. Remember that each thing we do reflects our integrity and our belief in God's love for us.

Whatever your goals are for today, take a step back, consider them prayerfully, and then aim a little higher.

A Taste of Self-control

Lord, help me to become an achiever of the highest caliber. Help me desire more of You in my life and help me set the bar higher in sharing more love with others. Amen.

Honest to God!

*May you receive more and more
of God's mercy, peace, and love.*

Jude 2 NLT

Try to stand in front of your bathroom mirror and say three nice things to yourself. What did you say?

If you couldn't think of three nice things to say to yourself, take an honest look at that. Being honest with yourself also means that you're being honest with God.

The idea behind this is not to get you to talk tenderly to yourself, although most of us need to do this more often. It's about getting to know who you are. If you don't know the truth about yourself, how can you expect others to really know who you are?

Go back to the mirror and take three deep breaths. Get acquainted with the person staring back at you and have an honest talk. This exercise could make the rest of your life more authentic and true.

A *Taste of Self-control*

Lord, help me to be honest with myself about the things that I believe and the choices I make. Above all, let me be honest with You. Amen.

Keep Smiling!

A cheerful look brings joy to the heart.
Proverbs 15:30 NLT

Have you noticed that when you offer the world a smile without hesitation or reservation, somehow your day feels lighter and brighter too?

The Eeyores of the world who always see the gloomy side of life, are there to remind us that a positive and cheerful disposition is indeed an exquisite gift.

When we assume life is hard, then more often than not, we experience difficulties. When we assume it is positive and joyful, we receive much more joy and delight. It's all about having the right attitude.

Today, expect nothing but sunshine and show your positive attitude. You're bound to cheer up perfect strangers and yourself as well.

A Taste of Joy

Lord, thank You for giving us so many wonderful things to experience in the world and help us create a day of delight today. Help me to remember to keep smiling for You. Amen.

Kind, in Deed!

Don't get tired of helping others. You will be rewarded when the time is right, if you don't give up. We should help people whenever we can, especially if they are followers of the Lord.
Galatians 6:9-10 CEV

Everywhere we go, we are blessed to meet strangers who may become friends. We are traveling the universe in a way that will help us understand the needs of others.

On our journey through life, we recognize the importance of kindness. Kindness is a universal language and can be spoken by anyone at any time. Kindness embraces weak souls and downhearted spirits. It is an action that can change an attitude in an instant and a secret ingredient of love to be employed every chance you get.

Don't ever weary of being kind. The reward is both instant and ongoing. Let every deed be one of kindness.

A Taste of Kindness

Lord, help me to remember that everyone I meet is fighting a battle of their own and a little kindness could inspire their hearts and minds today. Amen.

The Living Expression of God's Kindness

Dear children, let us stop just saying we love each other; let us really show it by our actions. It is by our actions that we know we are living in the truth, so we will be confident when we stand before the Lord.

1 John 3:18-19 NLT

Mother Teresa was indeed a saint in our time. She shared her love, her heart and her faith with people every day. Her words provided inspiration to those around her and are worth reading on a daily basis. She said:

"Spread love everywhere you go; first of all in your own house. Let no one ever come to you without leaving better and happier. Be the living expression of God's kindness; kindness in your face, kindness in your eyes, kindness in your smile, kindness in your warm greeting."

Can you imagine being the "living expression of God's kindness?" See today what you can do to be just that.

A Taste of Kindness

Lord, it is awesome to think about Your loving kindness and I thank You and praise You for such great love. Help me to share that love with others today. Amen.

The Kindness Business

*All of you should be of one mind, full of
sympathy toward each other, loving one another
with tender hearts and humble minds.*
1 Peter 3:8 NLT

Treating people well who do a job well is just as important as completing a job successfully. It's about the heart and not just the bottom line. Well, the bottom line for us is that kindness is always our business and we must never set it aside.

As the character of Scrooge says in Charles Dickens's, *Christmas Carol*, "Mankind is my business." Mankind, humankind, womankind, people kind ... that's our business! We need a heart like Christ's when dealing with people at any time.

Our job today is to cultivate kindness and to share a heart of sympathy and love with those we meet.

A Taste of Kindness
Lord, since I enjoy my life so much more when others are kind to me, remind me that I can return the favor today. Amen.

Committing Acts of Kindness

Be kind to each other, tenderhearted, forgiving one another,
just as God through Christ has forgiven you.
Ephesians 4:32 NLT

Kindness is a unique form of giving. It makes a big difference to both the giver and the receiver. Before you know it, your view of the world, your neighborhood, or your church begins to change and you see everyone as being more like you, rather than different from you. You realize that what the world needs is a little more kindness.

Rude, crude, mean and nasty have all been out there for some time at our expense. Isn't it time to combat them with big doses of kindness whenever you have the chance? Be part of the change you'd like to see in the world by committing random acts of kindness. It will make you feel good.

A Taste of Kindness

Lord, it's not hard to understand why kindness is indeed a fruit of the Spirit. You have brought incredible kindness to those You love and we're grateful for that. Amen.

Just Shine!

There are different kinds of spiritual gifts, but they all come from the same Spirit. There are different ways to serve the same Lord, and we can each do different things.
1 Corinthians 12:4-6 CEV

You probably have a pretty good idea by now of what your own special gifts are. The kind of insights and talents you offer to others are important and part of what attracts people to you. Your goal is to have expressed every talent God gave you by the time you return to Him.

If you don't know what your gifts are, then it's time to explore your passions, dreams and insights into life. You may identify talents you're not even aware of yet. Maybe you are a good speaker or tap dancer, but you won't know if you don't get out there and try.

Today shine and discover the gifts God gave you and enrich the lives of others by simply being you.

A Taste of Joy

Lord, I do experience great joy when I get to share my talents with my friends and family. I love doing the things You created me to do. Amen.

See Your Neighbor

"Love your neighbor as yourself."
Matthew 19:19

Do you ever feel slightly invisible? Do you wonder if anyone really knows who you are or how you actually feel about things? Isn't it strange that we often live in a neighborhood for years and scarcely know the people who live around us? We remain invisible to each other.

Your challenge today is to "see your neighbor." See if you can bring someone into the light of your life and your understanding and maybe let them see you in return. Find out the name of your mail carrier, or the paper boy. Practice making yourself and your neighbors more visible.

If you gently and sincerely practice getting to know those around you, you have greater opportunity to share your love and your joy in Jesus.

A Taste of Gentleness

Lord, it's not always easy to put myself out there to get to know people better, but I know how loneliness feels and I ask You to help me to be better at reaching out to others. Amen.

The Power of Kindness

*Do not withhold good from those who deserve it
when it's in your power to help them.*
Proverbs 3:27 NLT

Many of us assume that others, especially those who are wealthy or intelligent or in leadership positions, have power that we don't have. But are those seats of power really as strong as they appear to us?

The Talmud says, "There are ten strong things. Iron is strong, but fire melts it. Fire is strong, but water quenches it. Water is strong, but the clouds evaporate it. Clouds are strong, but wind drives them away. Man is strong, but fears cast him down. Fear is strong, but sleep overcomes it. Sleep is strong, yet death is stronger. But loving kindness survives death."

Perhaps the most powerful person you know is the neighbor who welcomes everyone to her table or the woman who loves with her whole heart.

Rekindle your own power today. The more you give away, the more you have.

A Taste of Kindness
Lord, help me understand what real power is in the world and pursue that power which is from the spirit of love. Amen.

Quiet Desperation

*Every good and perfect gift comes down from
the Father who created all the lights in the heavens.*
James 1:17 CEV

Henry David Thoreau said, "The mass of men lead lives of quiet desperation." Somehow that thought pales in comparison to the lives we were meant to live. Jesus promised us in John 10:10 that He came to give us life in abundance. What is the difference between having a life of quiet desperation and a life of abundance?

Some of the differences may simply lie in the attitude we bring to our circumstances. Desperation is about worry and the feeling that we have to close the door on possibility.

Since you're the child of a King, God wants to lavish you with love and all good things. He has a lot of gifts to give you and if you don't feel that you're receiving them, it may be that you need to sit a little closer to His throne.

A Taste of Faithfulness
Lord, thank You for the good things in my life. Amen.

Doing What Comes Naturally

It seems to be a fact of life that when I want to do
what is right, I inevitably do what is wrong.
Romans 7:21 NLT

It helps to list the things we want to accomplish because this will help us to get our work done. Sometimes though, we discover things on the list that we really don't want to do. When that happens, we're apt to procrastinate, or worse yet, just ignore the job completely. How can we prevent procrastination?

Start with an action. It gets things rolling and keeps you motivated to get the job done. The most significant action is simply to pray and align your activities with God right away so you'll be more likely to get them done. It also gives you the opportunity to invite God to be with you and to receive the blessings He brings when your work is done.

Pray every day and you'll find that more of your plans will succeed.

A Taste of Peace

Lord, help me to take the time to talk with You about what's on my list for the day. Bless my work in Your name. Amen.

Practicing Your Faith

Teach us to use wisely all the time we have.
Psalm 90:12 CEV

Each of us has learned certain practices to help us grow in our faith and become stronger and more fulfilled. St. Augustine's list is helpful even today.

- Order your soul – give priority to prayer and meditation
- Reduce your wants – learn to be content with what you have
- Live in charity – share what you have with those in need
- Associate in Christian community – spend time with fellow Christians
- Obey the laws – understand that we are all subject to the laws of our community and country
- Trust in Providence – trust, believe, and honor the God of your heart.

When you put these things into practice, you'll renew and refresh your faith every day.

A Taste of Faithfulness

Lord, help me to practice my faith in ways that will strengthen and renew my spirit. Amen.

Sometimes You Win!

*"If you love your life, you will lose it. If you give it
up in this world, you will be given eternal life."*
John 12:25 CEV

The Scripture presents life as a winning and losing
proposition. As a believer, you've already surrendered your life to Christ and are a winner.

Let's look at a few traits of a winner. Winners:

- are part of the answer; they don't add to the
  problem.
- find solutions; they don't find excuses.
- get things done themselves.
- say "yes" first.
- make the difficult possible; they don't make the
  possible difficult.
- start every task by surrendering it to God.

It's your day to win! Embrace the ways that God
would do things. You'll come out ahead.

A Taste of Faithfulness

Lord, help me be a winner today, according to Your
grace and mercy. Amen.

Check the Guidebook!

*The Spirit of God has made me, and the
breath of the Almighty gives me life.*
Job 33:4 NLT

Do you ever wish you had been born with some
kind of repair manual and guidebook? Then you
would know what to do when things get out of control in your life and where to go next.

Well, in a way, you were born with your own
manual. The manual might not have your name en-
graved on the cover, but I believe your name is actually in the book. We call the manual the Scriptures
and we look to them for help on practically every
issue we encounter.

You've probably thoroughly embraced your
manual by now, or maybe you think that you've
been here long enough not to need it anymore.

The truth is, you can't be around long enough to
really absorb all the details. You may still have a
thing or two to learn. Check the Guidebook today!

A Taste of Faithfulness

Lord, I read my Bible, but I don't always give it enough
time or turn to it when I have concerns. Remind me
that You've already provided some wonderful direction
for my life in those pages. Amen.

Over and Over Again

Everything that happens has happened before,
and all that will be has already been –
God does everything over and over again.
Ecclesiastes 3:15 CEV

Philosophers, theologians and scientists have been trying to explain the meaning of life for centuries. As humans we want life to have meaning.

King Solomon asked God for the gift of wisdom and God gave it to him with joy. After observing the world for some time, Solomon came to the conclusion that we should enjoy eating, drinking and working as a gift from God. If we please Him, He will give us wisdom, understanding and happiness (Eccles. 2:24-26).

Remember to enjoy making breakfast, listening to the birds, hugging your children and sharing moments with a friend. Rejoice in knowing we can do it over and over again!

A Taste of Gentleness
Lord, let me always draw more meaning from life in Your Presence. Amen.

Chasing the Wind

*It's better to enjoy what we have than always
to want something else, because that
makes no more sense than chasing the wind.*

Ecclesiastes 6:9 CEV

Let's step outside and try to catch the wind. What shall we catch it in? What about a net or a plastic bag? Right, to catch the wind will be very difficult. Are there places in your life where you are chasing the wind?

It's good to go after new things and to keep growing. Sometimes though, we get caught in our own net trying to chase dreams that we haven't turned over to God.

Today, before you go running about, stop and check the Guidebook, then check with the Guide Himself and ask Him to help you to find the joy in all you have before you chase the wind and go after something else.

A Taste of Patience

Lord, remind me to be thankful for all that I have at this very moment, and to look to You for help in all that is still mine to explore. Amen.

Worth Remembering

*"The eye is the lamp of the body. If your eyes
are good, your whole body will be full of light."*

Matthew 6:22

Sometimes it's good to start the day by simply
thinking of a few worthwhile things. Here are a few
to get you started. Your:

- kindness brings power
- wisdom brings peace
- heart brings love
- work brings joy
- perseverance brings patience
- helping hand brings gentleness
- prayer life brings self-control
- daily Bible reading brings goodness
- desire to please God brings faithfulness

Your day is blessed by the fruit of the Spirit and
your life is in God's hand. Let your head, your heart,
and your eyes be full of light.

A *Taste of Joy*

Lord, thank You for bringing real joy into my life through
the gifts of Your ever-present Spirit. Amen.

Worth Forgetting

Pride leads to disgrace, but with humility comes wisdom.
Proverbs 11:2 NLT

It is important to remember things that motivate you to grow and to become strong. Think about the following:

* Self-criticism – a little goes a long way
* Worry – hand it over to God instead
* Embarrassment – everybody has done something to blush about
* Pride – it has never served you well
* Gossip – a little goes a lot further than you expect
* Anger – misdirected anger will not serve you well
* Doubt – a little of this will totally mislead you
* Procrastination – will never let you get things cleared up
* Revenge – let God take care of things.

Most of these are not things you do anyway, but sometimes it's helpful to look at the things you can simply let go.

A Taste of Self-control

Lord, help me to let go of those things that only cause further pain and unhappiness in my life. Let me surrender all those things to You today. Amen.

Standing in the Light!

*The One who is the true light, who gives light
to everyone, was going to come into the world.*
John 1:9 NLT

Albert Schweitzer once said, "Your life is something opaque, not transparent, as long as you look at it in an ordinary human way. But if you hold it up against the light of God's goodness, it shines and turns transparent, radiant and bright. And then you ask yourself in amazement. Is this really my own life I see before me?'"

Try holding your life closer to the light of God's goodness. See if you radiate more joy as you recognize all He has done to give you peace and pleasure. You are His incredible light in the world and He wants you to stand in utter delight in every way possible. Shine for Him today!

A Taste of Joy

Lord, I am so grateful for Your constant beam of light that brings such joy to my life. Never let me get too far from Your utter brilliance! Amen.

Everlasting Shine!

Many people say, "Who will show us better times?"
Let the smile of Your face shine on us, LORD.
You have given me greater joy than those who
have abundant harvests of grain and wine.

Psalm 4:6-7 NLT

If you're seeking better times and greater joy in your life, then there's only one place to get the kind of shine that simply won't fade or go out of vogue or lose its luster. In fact, this is the Light of lights and you're already basking in it.

Imagine today that you have the radiating smile of God's face shining down on you. That incredible love is focused on you. It gives you greater joy than all the jewels at Tiffany's. You've got the best and the brightest and it feels good.

If you've stepped back into the shadows today, then it's time to come back out into the light and give God the glory. You're set to sparkle!

A Taste of Joy

Lord, there is nothing more wonderful than sharing in Your light. Thanks for giving me so many good things. Amen.

Light Show

*"Make your light shine, so that others will see the good
that you do and will praise your Father in heaven."*
Matthew 5:16 CEV

As a child of God, you have light to share and others are in need of it. You may be a candle, the floodlight, the flashlight, something that shines directly on those around you. You may also simply hold up the mirror of grace and with genuine kindness and goodness, share the light of your faith with others.

The point is that you don't have to be an evangelist or a church leader to be a beacon to those in need. You just have to be willing to let your light shine so that others will know the Source of your joy and inspiration.

Today, see if you can be a candle of inspiration, a beam of joy, a twinkle of blessing to someone around you. It can make a big difference.

A Taste of Goodness

Lord, help me to radiate Your light in positive, warm and loving ways to those I spend time with today. Amen.

Child of Light

*You are all children of the light and of the day;
we don't belong to darkness and night.*
1 Thessalonians 5:5 NLT

Read this proverb and consider how you can be a child of light today.

*If there is light in the soul,
there will be beauty in the person.
If there is beauty in the person,
there will be harmony in the house.
If there is harmony in the house,
there will be order in the nation.
If there is order in the nation,
there will be peace in the world.*

We should reflect the Light of the world's love and truth and carry it within ourselves to find God's peace. Let this light create harmony in all that you do today and illuminate the way for everyone you see.

A Taste of Gentleness
Lord, help me to gently and freely and lovingly shine Your light today for the sake of each person I meet. Amen.

Genuine Love

You must teach people to have genuine love,
as well as a good conscience and true faith.
1 Timothy 1:5 CEV

Most of us think we understand what love is and what it is all about, and yet a quick look around the world might make us wonder how much we really know about the subject.

Perhaps the problem rests in genuine love, versus artificial love. There's a lot of love being bandied about as though it could be the real thing in ads and TV shows and even relationships. We may still need some further education.

Starting with what you know about God's love, or the love shared in your family, spend some time this week and concentrate on the word, the idea, the concept of love. Study it until you get to the place where you can identify genuine love over all imitations. The lesson may well be worth the effort.

A Taste of Love

Lord, help me to understand Your love in such a way that I can use that as a measure for how I need to love and how I hope to be loved in return. Amen.

Neighbors and Strangers

"Love your neighbor as yourself."
Mark 12:31

If you've been living in your community for a long time, chances are pretty good that you know some of your neighbors and have a nodding acquaintance with many of them.

We tend to think that love is an emotional response between two people, or a response of one person toward something else, like chocolate, for instance.

Now, if you don't know your neighbors, or the neighbors next to them, or the ones across town, how are you supposed to love them? How do you love your neighbor as yourself?

Perhaps one way is to expand your understanding of what it means to be a neighbor, and another is to simply get to know your neighbors better. You will obtain some important insights as to how you can then love them.

A Taste of Kindness

Lord, it's not easy to make the effort to love people I don't know. I have enough trouble with the people I do know. Help me to be a better neighbor. Amen.

You were Meant to Shine!

*"You are like light for the whole world ... Make
your light shine, so that others will see the good
that you do and will praise your Father in heaven."*
Matthew 5:14, 16 CEV

In the middle of the day the stars and moon are still shining, they just step back for the sun. They wait for their turn to reflect more joy.

You're a little like that too. Your light is always available, but often it shines best in the darkness. You were designed to fill the dark spaces and bring them light. You're like a switch being turned on so everyone can see more clearly. You send your waves of love and grace out into the world and hope that the darkness will embrace your message.

As a child of God, you carry the light to every corner of the globe. You can reflect Him like the moon and shine for everyone to see, or shine His light like the sunshine and bring His warmth to those in great need of it.

You were made to shine!

A Taste of Goodness
Lord, it is such an honor to share Your grace and Your light with others. Amen.

Producing Lasting Fruit

*"You didn't choose Me. I chose you. I appointed you
to go and produce fruit that will last, so that
the Father will give you whatever you ask for,
using My name. I command you to love each other."*
John 15:16-17 NLT

You have been chosen out of many people to shine a very special light. When you gave your heart to the Lord, you told Him you were interested in moving His cause forward. He looked at the jobs that needed to be done and He said, "I want you!"

How are you doing with your part? Do you need to rehearse your lines more so you're ready for the biggest event yet? The answer is yes! You need to prepare for the part you are playing because what you do makes a difference and you have to produce fruit that will last.

Today, see what you can do to improve your role. After all, you were chosen and that makes you pretty special indeed!

A Taste of Self-control

Lord, help me today to prepare myself to be a better light. Grant me insights into Your Word and in my prayers. Let me shine for You. Amen.

The Spirit of Truth

*"When the Spirit of truth comes,
He will guide you into all truth."*
John 16:13 NLT

Most of us spend a lot of time beating ourselves up over poor decisions and past sins. Then we spend a lot of time worrying about the future and wondering if we'll have any success with our dreams. We sometimes totally forget to actually live and let God help us one day at a time.

All we have to do is ask the Spirit of Truth to share with us all that the Father has in mind. He can give us some insight into the future. Isn't that pretty incredible?

If you're limping along today, wondering if life is ever going to get where you want it to go, then stop what you're doing and surrender to the guidance of the Spirit of Truth. You'll receive some very clear answers.

A Taste of Faithfulness

Lord, it is awesome that You have provided so well for our needs. You know everything about us and we need only come to You to claim our joy. Help me seek the Spirit of Truth today. Amen.

Love Yourself, Come on, You Can Do It!

"Love others as much as you love yourself."
Mark 12:31 CEV

How you feel about yourself at any particular time has a lot to do with how loving you are to everyone else. On days when you're feeling good about yourself you're willing to be giving, forgiving and generous.

When you're down and you constantly judge yourself harshly, you treat people a little less kindly. It seems that to improve this situation you must get better at loving yourself.

Maybe you need to give yourself a break and see if you can discover why God loves you in the first place. Once you realize that if God loves you, you can't be so bad, then maybe you'll see that you can carry that love to others.

Today love yourself. When you love yourself you will be able to love others.

A Taste of Love
Lord, You know I'm not very good at seeing the positive and lovable things about myself. Help me to love myself the way You do and then help me to love others too. Amen.

Keep Love Growing

*May the Lord make your love for each other and
for everyone else grow by leaps and bounds.*
1 Thessalonians 3:12 CEV

Love demands action. It isn't content to sit passively by, while everyone else is playing the game. In fact, love usually wants to shout out its existence to everyone as much as possible. If it's just quiet and demure, then love may not be feeling well.

When you think about your love for God, it should make you feel happy and good and demand some action from you. Is there some small way that you can show God your love today?

If you let your love grow and become more active, you may find yourself smiling a bit more and getting more excited about life because that's what love does when it's actively growing!

A Taste of Love

Lord, I'm so thankful for the opportunities I have to grow in Your love and Your sunshine. Help me to act on that love in every possible way. Amen.

Love Does Not Compute!

Love is more important than anything else.
It is what ties everything completely together.
Colossians 3:14 CEV

When we think of romantic love we generally think that one plus one equals two – who together become one. Funny math, but somehow we get it. If we then add God's love we form a three-fold cord which makes the relationship even stronger.

That's how it is when everything is going well but we're often left wondering why love just does not compute.

Maybe the best way to compute love is to strive for the greatest love you can imagine and assign a number to it. God's love is a million gazillion. You'll be seeing love everywhere you go if you do this.

In the mathematics of love, the more you give away, the more you have left. Try to give more away.

A Taste of Love

Lord, remind me that I am loved and that I have a lot of love around me all the time. Help me to compute love and compound it with interest. Amen.

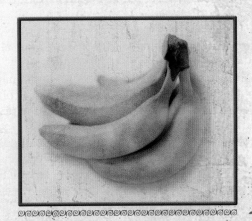

November

Blessing our Differences

*Each one of you is part of the body of Christ,
and you were chosen to live together in peace.*
Colossians 3:15 CEV

We are all different, but the truth is we're more alike than we are different.

We live in a world that applauds our unique gifts and talents and that's a good thing. It often gives rise to competitive attitudes and in the realm of perfecting our skills, that's good too.

However, we all have the same essential needs and we try to create the best environment to have those needs fulfilled. It's our duty to become all that God created us to be, and we have a duty to each other to share God's grace and Spirit.

As Christ's representatives, on earth, part of our mission is to share the Good News! Today as you strive to become the best *you* that you can be, strive also to become more for Him.

A Taste of Self-control
Lord, thank You for the many gifts You've given me. Help me to share those gifts in ways that will glorify You. Amen.

It's About Love

Most important of all, continue to show deep love for each other, for love covers a multitude of sins.
1 Peter 4:8 NLT

Have you ever been walking along and thought something similar to, "Someone needs to help them pick out their clothes!" It's not a terrible judgment, but a judgment just the same and before you know it, you lob another one at someone else.

Mother Teresa said, "If you judge people, you have no time to love them." It's a good thought. We can easily determine the way other people should live their lives, as though we actually know, and not ever lift a hand to share God's love.

The fruit of the Spirit is love. Judging isn't really our job. Loving is! As you go about your day today, stop yourself any time some little judgment is about to slip out and send a prayer of love instead. Better yet, extend the hand of God's fellowship.

A Taste of Love

Lord, I'm so critical about myself that I know I tend to do the same things to others without even thinking. Help me to be more loving both to those around me and to myself. Amen.

Putting up with Each Other!

God loves you and has chosen you as His own special
people. So be gentle, kind, humble, meek, and patient.
Put up with each other, and forgive anyone who
does you wrong, just as Christ has forgiven you.
Colossians 3:12-13 CEV

It's interesting to read a phrase like "put up with each other" in Scripture. It usually means one of us is pretty sure we're right and we're "putting up with the other". Or it could be that someone is "putting up with you!"

Either way, this verse helps us see that gentleness and humility are hallmarks that should let us give each other room to be who we are. Isn't that really what we all want? It's all part of recognizing that God loves us just the way we are and He expects us to love each other that way too.

If you need to be kinder, gentler, or more humble, this might be a good day to work on these things.

A Taste of Gentleness

Lord, help me to remember that other people put up with me just as often as I put up with them. Whatever I do today, help me to be full of Your kindness and love. Amen.

A Cup of Sugar, Please!

*Let love be your highest goal, but also desire
the special abilities the Spirit gives.*
1 Corinthians 14:1 NLT

You have company coming in fifteen minutes and you think you have everything set and then you realize the sugar bowl is empty. Those are the moments you're so grateful for good neighbors!

Looking at this another way, we may also run into a snag in our thinking if we assume that because we only have a cup of sugar to offer, it doesn't really count. The truth is that it all counts. Each thing we do for each other out of kindness or joy or genuine willingness is a gift of the Spirit. It's part of our gentleness and joy and is not to be overlooked. Think about how happy you feel when someone does some special kindness for you.

If all you have today is a cup of sugar to share, then sprinkle it among as many friends and neighbors as you can. You'll sweeten everyone's lives.

A Taste of Goodness

Lord, help me to give from whatever I have, any time the need arises. Amen.

Love Talk

*If I could speak in any language in heaven or on earth
but didn't love others, I would only be making
meaningless noise like a loud gong or a clanging cymbal.*

1 Corinthians 13:1 NLT

When we are involved in various everyday activities there is one thing to remember. We need to do everything with a heart for others. We need to do everything in love. We can have a Ph.D. in amazing areas of science, or math or linguistics, but the language we speak and the work we do has no meaning apart from what our hearts are also doing. If you're heart isn't connected to your work, you may as well be a "clanging cymbal".

We take pride in our successes and that's okay, as long as our goals are aligned with God's purpose and our hearts are reaching out to others. Listen carefully to yourself today. Are you a clanging cymbal or a symphony of love?

A Taste of Love

Lord, let me remember always that my real work involves loving those You've brought into my life. Amen.

Worth Waiting For

The LORD is wonderfully good to those who wait
for Him and seek Him. So it is good to
wait quietly for salvation from the LORD.
Lamentations 3:25-26 NLT

There are always a few decisions that need to be made that can be life changing. When you're figuring out whether to take a new job in a city that will take you away from your family or how to invest your savings, what you decide can change your life.

How do you determine your course of action? "Patient endurance is what you need now, so you will continue to do God's will. Then you will receive all that He has promised" (Heb. 10:36, NLT).

Waiting on God's promise with patient endurance often feels more like endurance than simply waiting. Your next important decision may be worth some patient endurance to see what the Lord has in mind. He will truly direct your steps if you give Him a chance.

A Taste of Patience

Lord, it is not unusual for me to leap ahead of You and forget about waiting to hear what You would have me do. Help me today to wait patiently for You to help me make good choices. Amen.

The Shifting Shadows

Whatever is good and perfect comes to us from God above, who created all heaven's lights. Unlike them, He never changes or casts shifting shadows.
James 1:17 NLT

You might know someone who is cheerful one day and suddenly extremely depressed the next day.

Your life can be like that too. It seems to be going along fine, rain or shine, and everything feels safe and secure. Then before you know it, everything has shifted and you can't figure out which end is up.

The one thing that doesn't have to change is your outlook on these events. You can know exactly how you're going to approach them and what you're going to do because your attitude is based on the constant faith that you have in Jesus Christ. Build your day on the Rock, and you won't have to worry when the sands of change start shifting under your feet.

A Taste of Self-control

Lord, help me to look to You when things around me seem out of control. Help me to see my life as being steady and strong in Your hand. Amen.

Adding to Your Style

Clothe yourselves with tenderhearted mercy, kindness, hu-mility, gentleness, and patience. You must make allowance for each other's faults and forgive the person who offends you.

Colossians 3:12-13 NLT

Patience serves as a protection against wrongs as clothes do against cold. For if you put on more clothes as the cold increases, it will have no power to hurt you. So in like man-ner, you must grow in patience when you meet with great wrongs, and they will be powerless to vex your mind.

~ Leonardo da Vinci

In the same way you layer clothes, you can layer patience. Think of patience as a scarf you always have with you to put on when things start to irritate you and to protect yourself enough to stay calm. It's not always easy to be dressed just right for every contingency, but with the scarf of patience, you'll be less apt to come unraveled throughout the day.

A *Taste of Patience*
Lord, I can come undone pretty easily when little things pile up and irritate me. Help me prepare for those things and dress my spirit in patience. Amen.

The Patience of Job

There was a man named Job who lived in the land of Uz.
He was blameless, a man of complete integrity.

Job 1:1 NLT

Fortunately, most of us have only had to deal with a few of Job's devastating life experiences. We've suffered losses of health, or jobs, or family, or friends, or respect, but not all of those things.

The lesson from Job is that spiritual warfare continues. We may not see all the land mines out there that try to hinder our walk with God, but He does and we must pay close attention.

Remaining faithful can be a challenge. If you've had to face miseries over and over again, you can begin to wonder if God really knows you're there. The answer is that He does know and He cares. Embrace the challenges, believe in yourself, and know that all good things will be restored to you soon.

A Taste of Patience

Lord, it is so hard to always be patient! When life keeps handing me one bad news report after another, I hardly know what to believe. Help me to keep believing in You with all my heart. Amen.

How Do You Spell Patience?

You will show me the way of life, granting me the joy of Your presence and the pleasures of living with You forever.
Psalm 16:11 NLT

On those days when you simply have no extra time to get things done, something usually happens that makes it impossible to complete your To-do list.

When this happens, you need to stop, take a deep breath and think about what you can do while the impulse toward negative thinking looms. Let's look at it in terms of the word PATIENCE itself.

- P – stands for peace, prayer and positive spirit
- A – stands for attitude adjustment
- T – stands for thankfulness for all you have
- I – stands for insight and imitating Christ
- E – stands for expecting that all is well
- N – stands for not giving in to negative thoughts
- C – stands for caring about all those around you
- E – stands for experiencing more of God's grace

When you find yourself being vexed, pull out your patience card and walk through each step. God will make sure all your needs are met.

A Taste of Patience
Lord, be with me today as I work through the things that keep me from being patient. Amen.

Bookmark This!

"May the LORD be good to you and give you peace."
Numbers 6:26 CEV

Peace is a beautiful word and Teresa of Avila offered a bit of wisdom on the subject of peace centuries ago:

> Let nothing disturb you,
> nothing frighten you,
> all things pass
> and God never changes.
> When you endure things with patience,
> you attain all things that God can give you.
> When you have God,
> you lack for nothing.

Peace is to be found in God. We may not find it in all situations as they exist here on earth, but we can find it in the place we also find safety and rest ... in the arms of our Savior.

A Taste of Peace
Lord, grant me Your wonderful sense of peace today and let me share that peace with each one I meet. Amen.

Power to the Peacemakers!

*"God blesses those people who make peace.
They will be called His children!"*
Matthew 5:9 CEV

We live in a world that is at war all the time and with governments that are run by greed and power.

In such a situation, how do children of God become powerful peacemakers when we're not sitting in the seats of power? How can we be counted as peacekeepers? We become warriors of prayer and vigilantly pray for peace in the world, in our communities and in the hearts of every person. We surrender our need for things and embrace our need for each other. We become Samaritans knowing that life itself depends on us and leaders who will defend the good and create a place for future generations to exist.

Let peace rule in your heart today and then find a moment to pray for peace until the victory is won.

A Taste of Peace

Lord, I know that many of Your children do not live so peacefully. Remind me to pray for peace every day. Amen.

The Dance of Peace

*May grace and peace be yours, sent to you from
God our Father and Jesus Christ our Lord.*

Ephesians 1:2 NLT

In some cultures dance is a common way to worship. It is used to both glorify God and to seek His help. Perhaps we should pull out our dancing shoes and offer a special prayer for peace in every community in the world. Children of God could come together as representatives of all of humanity and ask for His direction in the efforts for peace that are going on everywhere in the world.

It doesn't matter what kind of dancer you are or whether you have the right outfit or the right dance partner. You simply need to have the desire to see peace happen in our time and in our own community. Sing, dance, pray ... it's about creating an action that will keep your heart and mind focused on peace. It's time to get in step! Create peace today!

A Taste of Peace

Lord, I'm sure I'm not a good dancer, but I'm a good prayer and I lift my voice and tap my feet with my brothers and sisters around the world, asking for Your gift of peace. Amen.

Bits of Wisdom

Proverbs will teach you wisdom and self-control and how to understand sayings with deep meanings.
Proverbs 1:2 CEV

Advertisers count on their slogans to make you remember their product and persuade you to buy it. It seems that beyond the advertising world, every culture, faith system and specialty group has some sort of tag line that helps make them seem utterly familiar and inviting.

Proverbs are helpful in that regard too. They may come from the Bible or they may come from anywhere around the world but simply put, they offer bits of wisdom that we can find useful.

Invest a little time today exploring the Proverbs and commit one or two to memory. It will surely serve you well. As Proverbs 1:7 says, "Respect and obey the LORD! This is the beginning of knowledge. Only a fool rejects wisdom and good advice!"

A Taste of Self-control
Lord, grant me wisdom in understanding more of the things that will help me live a life that honors You and those around me. Amen.

A Little Common Sense

Keep in tune with wisdom and think what it
means to have common sense. Beg as loud as you
can for good common sense. Search for wisdom
as you would search for silver or hidden treasure.

Proverbs 2:2-4 CEV

Does it seem like we've almost gotten too smart and sophisticated to be able to actually do the sensible and sometimes simple things? We're in such pursuit of brilliant, lofty ideas and can totally lose sight of every day, garden-variety common sense.

This Scripture is wonderful in its approach. "Beg as loud as you can for good common sense," it says. It seems like even God knows we are apt to lose track of it and that we'll have to call on Him to get it back. If you're able to explain quantum theory but can't figure out your checkbook, you're in a position to start begging ... loudly!

Today observe whether you're balancing your own act with the right degree of common sense. If you're not ... beg for more. You'll be glad you did.

A Taste of Self-control

Lord, I admit that I don't always do things in the most sensible way. Help me to remember that a little more common sense would be a good thing to seek. Amen.

Advice about Advice

*Without good advice everything goes wrong –
it takes careful planning for things to go right.*
Proverbs 15:22 CEV

When we're asked to give advice, we're often uncertain as to whether we really should tell someone what we think. This is especially true if what we think is contrary to what we believe they think.

When we're seeking advice, we're more open to it, unless we're just seeking confirmation of our own direction, and then it's hardly advice that will meet our needs anyway. We must seek to offer and to receive the best advice we can in love because part of our mission in being God's people is to listen with ears attuned to the Holy Spirit, and to speak with a voice that is pleasing to God.

We are God's voice and often our advice can bring His desire to someone's attention. After prayerful consideration, give your best advice with love.

A Taste of Kindness

Lord, help me to offer advice in a loving way when asked, and to seek advice from those who will help guide me according to Your will and purpose. Amen.

Today, Well Lived!

Don't boast about tomorrow!
Each day brings its own surprises.
Proverbs 27:1 CEV

"Look to this day ... In it lie all the realities and verities of existence, the bliss of growth, the splendor of action, the glory of power. For yesterday is but a dream and tomorrow is only a vision. But today, well lived, makes every yesterday a dream of happiness and every tomorrow a vision of hope."
~ Sanskrit proverb

Most days we hardly think about whether we'll accomplish anything truly meaningful or whether the day will bring happiness.

But were we to think about the prize, which is a day well lived, then perhaps we'd look for more and find more. Yesterday cannot be reclaimed. Who knows what tomorrow will bring?

Today is what God has given you. Today He has offered you the world and He will rejoice if you live it well. Don't miss today, it is a gift to you.

A Taste of Joy
Lord, thank You for loving me so much and giving me the gift of today. Help me to use it wisely and live it well. Amen.

Prayers of Faith

The prayer of an innocent person is powerful.
James 5:16 CEV

When most of us pray, we come humbly before God, seeking guidance, solace and forgiveness. We come to Him on our knees because we are so grateful that He hears our requests and honors them.

However, we often wonder why our request does not seem to be answered or if God even heard what we had to say because the answer does not come in a form we expected.

We must pray believing. What does that mean? It means that when we pray, we must pray as though the answer is already before us because in truth it is. God often answers before we even ask because He knows so well what we need.

Your mission today is not simply to pray, but to pray with such belief that great things happen. As you align your spirit with God's Spirit, you allow Him to create great answers through you.

A Taste of Faithfulness

Lord, help my unbelief. Help me to know and to believe that You desire my heartfelt prayers and that You answer them with joy. Amen.

The Believing Heart

*"Everything you ask for in prayer
will be yours, if you only have faith."*
Mark 11:24 CEV

Prayer is a heart thing. The real truth of prayer rests between you and God. It concerns your heart, your motivation and your faith. God hears and honors all your prayers, but He can do a lot more for you when you have no doubt and are fully prepared to receive the gifts and blessings you ask for.

Doubt blocks the way of His answers. If doubt is clogging up your prayer mechanism, then you're making it very difficult for Him to have enough room to act your behalf.

Remember, if you're willing to pray, God is willing to answer. Nothing is too big or too small for God. Ask God for greater faith and read the Word to strengthen your spirit. It's a new day to pray and God is waiting to hear your prayers.

A Taste of Faithfulness
Lord, I do believe You're listening when I pray, but I sometimes struggle with believing that my concerns really matter. Thank You for loving me just the way I am. Amen.

Please Hold!

"Everyone who asks will receive. Everyone who searches will find. And the door will be opened for everyone who knocks."
Matthew 7:7-8 CEV

We live in a busy world and when you try to call a company for information the first thing you hear is, "Please hold." If you're lucky, you get through to the party you wanted, but just as often, you have to leave a message.

God does not put you on hold! When you search for Him, He answers. He is always available and you don't even need to go through a switchboard operator. When you call, He answers directly.

If you're waiting for answers, keep asking and you will receive. Believe and knock louder. Give God time to answer. It is not that He didn't hear you immediately when you put in your request, but sometimes you and He have to work on the answer together.

Give Him a call ... His line is open to you.

A Taste of Faithfulness

Lord, I'm grateful just to know You're there when I call. I'll wait humbly for Your answers because only You know what is best for my life. Amen.

The Heart of Prayer

We also pray that you will be strengthened with
His glorious power so that you will have
all the patience and endurance you need.

Colossians 1:11 NLT

You may not always be in the mood to pray, but once you begin to pray, your heart will reshape and fit the mood perfectly. Mother Teresa said, "Love to pray. Feel often during the day the need for prayer, and take the trouble to pray. Prayer enlarges the heart until it is capable of containing God's gift of Himself. Ask and seek and your heart will grow big enough to receive Him."

What a wonderful thought! Prayer itself will expand your heart so that you can receive all that God intends just for you. Your heart is all that's needed for real prayer to happen, for a connection to be made. God sees your heart and comes to relieve and receive and bless its desires.

A Taste of Love

Lord, prayer is about love. Prayer is about the heart. Help me to love You so much that I bring everything to You in prayer. Amen.

Who Can Stop the Rain?

The eyes of the Lord watch over those who do right,
and His ears are open to their prayers.
1 Peter 3:12 NLT

This verse from Peter reminds us that when we do what is right in God's eyes, He is there to hear our requests.

Prayer is part of "doing right." Another part of prayer is simply believing that God hears and that He does indeed answer when you call. Expecting an answer in faith means you have to chase any doubts away.

Elijah, the ancient prophet prayed that it would not rain and it didn't rain for three and a half years. Then he prayed again for rain and the heavens opened up and the crops were restored. He believed that God would honor his prayer.

Like Elijah you may have a definite need for God to be with you and answer a fervent prayer. Keep your umbrella handy because you will receive what you pray for if you believe.

A Taste of Faithfulness

Lord, I know You're listening but I never know for sure if I'm praying about the right things. Help me to align my prayers and heart with You. Amen.

Either Talk or Action

So, my dear brothers and sisters, be strong and steady,
always enthusiastic about the Lord's work, for you
know that nothing you do for the Lord is ever useless.
1 Corinthians 15:58 NLT

Have you ever been part of a group or even around a person who means well, or intends to do things for others, but somehow never actually gets to it? If all the talkers were put in a room, probably one doer would complete the task before they took a break for donuts and coffee.

God wants us to be doers. He wants us to serve one another with love and joy and a sense of connection to Him. He wants us to get past the discussion of what we will do and get out there and do something. The truth is, it doesn't work at all if you don't do it.

Serving others is like that. Gather information so you know where to start, pray about the opportunities, trust that the doors will be open and serve.

A Taste of Goodness
Lord, I know that I often mean to help out and somehow don't get around to it. Help me to serve with a willing and happy heart. Amen.

Making Life Count

*You should be happy to give the poor what
they need, because then the LORD will
make you successful in everything you do.*
Deuteronomy 15:10 CEV

Most of us have a great desire for our lives to have
meaning and purpose and to know that we have a
positive impact on those around us. God gives us
that opportunity every day. We can share our gifts,
skills, talents and money with others.

In this regard Emily Dickinson said:

*If I can stop one heart from breaking,
I shall not live in vain;
If I can ease one life the aching,
Or cool one pain.
Or help one fainting robin
Unto his nest again,
I shall not live in vain.*

You can make life count for someone today.
Show them your goodness and compassion.

A Taste of Goodness
Lord, I often think about those in need and I do my best
to help, but I know I don't do it enough. Please let me
live more abundantly in Your service. Amen.

Christ has No Body ... but Yours!

*There is one body and one Spirit – just as you were
called to one hope when you were called – one Lord,
one faith, one baptism; one God and Father of all.*
Ephesians 4:4-6

You may not always recognize your value but God
always does. He does because He can't get His work
done nearly as well without you.

You're part of the body of Christ and you signed
up the day you accepted Jesus as your Lord and
Savior.

Teresa of Avila said, "Christ has no body now on
earth but yours; yours are the only hands with
which He can do His work, yours are the only feet
with which He can go about the world, yours are
the only eyes through which His compassion can
shine forth upon a troubled world. Christ has no
body on earth but yours."

Do you see how important you are?

A Taste of Love

Lord, help me to be Your hands and feet today. Help me
to love as You would love each one You meet. Amen.

Making the Effort

*You should work all the harder because you
are helping another believer by your efforts.*
1 Timothy 6:2 NLT

On a committee there are always people who do
what is asked of them and they are very consistent.
Then there are go-getters who seem to get the job
done almost single-handedly. Finally, there are
those who attend the meetings but never seem to
have a clue about what they can do to help.

Everywhere these three types of people are
somewhere in the mix. Add to the mix the person
who feels that the old ways of doing things have
always worked and therefore change isn't needed.

Whichever person you are, pray for God's guidance and grace to direct your steps as you serve Him
and others. There's room for you and He knows exactly what your role is and what needs to be done
today.

A Taste of Self-control
Lord, help me to be of real value to any situation
– whether I'm on a committee or sharing time with
my family. Let me make the effort out of love for You.
Amen.

Opening a Can of Success

A longing fulfilled is sweet to the soul.
Proverbs 13:19

Living in a world of instant gratification means that we have a pretty high expectation that we can attain things fairly easily. We buy a can of soup, take it home, pop it in the microwave oven in its own ready made bowl, and sit down to eat it.

We tend to think things should come fairly easily and sometimes our frustration in prayer or getting God's guidance is that He doesn't always give in to our "instant gratification" life. Sometimes He wants us to learn a few special things along the way.

Success does come in cans however. It can be opened every time you say to God, "Yes, I can do that." Each time you believe you can accomplish something, you're that much closer to making it really happen.

A Taste of Self-control

Lord, I do want to be successful in doing the work You've called me to do. Help me believe that I can do all things through You. Amen.

Dreams of Success

*Commit to the L*ORD *whatever you do,*
and your plans will succeed.
Proverbs 16:3

Dreams are the motivators, the gift givers. They help you determine your goals and with the grace of God, you have a chance to reach them.

However some dreamers create a scenario of how they will develop a dream and assume that each thing must be in place before they can actually take a step toward their goal. Why? Most of the time perfection can almost guarantee that the person won't have to take the risk of actually going after the dream. The dream can just be a vision of sugarplums.

If you're dreaming for an outcome of something you really want, don't set up roadblocks that will make it impossible. Set your prayers and your heart before God and commit your dreams to Him. The outcome will be assured.

A Taste of Self-control

Lord, I know that I am often my worst enemy when it comes to completing the things that I dream about. Help me overcome my own fears and go after the dreams of my heart. Amen.

What it Means to Succeed

*As long as he sought the L*ORD*, God gave him success.*
2 Chronicles 26:5

Sometimes we believe that success has something to do with money or power or position. You have to wonder though if that would be God's measure of success.

Ralph Waldo Emerson said, "Success: To laugh often and much, to win the respect of intelligent people and the affection of children, to earn the appreciation of honest critics and endure the betrayal of false friends, to appreciate beauty, to find the best in others, to know even one life has breathed easier because you lived. This is to have succeeded."

If your goals have something to do with leaving the world a bit better than you found it, or sharing love with at least one other soul, then you can count yourself among the successful. As you seek the Lord, He will continue to give you glorious opportunities to succeed.

A Taste of Goodness
Lord, the real fruit of the Spirit is always to show Your love, for that is where real success emanates. Help me to succeed in ways that please You today. Amen.

Finding the Rainbow

*"I am giving you a sign as evidence of My
eternal covenant with you and all living creatures.
I have placed My rainbow in the clouds."*
Genesis 9:12-13 NLT

After being sealed up in the ark for months, it had to be a welcome sight to Noah to see the rainbow appear in the sky.

Oftentimes we're in great need of a rainbow to motivate us. God is busy planning your future. He sees the rain coming into your life, but He's preparing a place in the sun for you.

As you patiently wait for God, open the doors to every opportunity for Him to enter your life. Let Him wash your concerns away and create a bright new day for you. You will come upon your rainbow when you least expect it. Your Father has already placed it in the clouds.

A Taste of Patience
Lord, it is so hard for me to wait for Your direction sometimes and especially when things in my life are just not coming together as I'm expecting. Send me Your rainbow today. Amen.

December

Buzz! Thank You for Playing!

Be an example to all believers in what you teach, in the way you live, in your love, your faith, and your purity.
1 Timothy 4:12 NLT

When it comes to choices and new opportunities, life is like a game show. You simply press the buzzer saying 'Game over, thank you for playing' and move on to the next opportunity. To approach life like that makes it easier to get back to the winning side of things.

The Sponsor of your game show is very interested in your choices and wants you to do the right thing. Part of living is about making choices, and we don't have to beat ourselves up if a choice doesn't pan out the way we had hoped. We simply need to have the faith and the courage to move on.

Be an example to everyone around you and take each new choice as an opportunity for you and God to create an absolutely new game plan.

A Taste of Self-control

Lord, I'm always a little hesitant to make new choices. I seem to lose as often as I win. Help me to remember to put more of my choices in Your hand. Amen.

The Bear Went Over the Mountain

We live by believing and not by seeing.
2 Corinthians 5:7 NLT

In the silly song *The Bear Went Over the Mountain* he did so to "see what he could see."

Sometimes we too need a new perspective on things to be able to get a grander view before we can go on and get our lives together. G. K. Chesterton said, "One sees great things from the valley; only small things from the peak."

That could mean that we have to "go over the mountain" before we can actually see all the great things that are there for us to discover. We have to look up into the hills from the valley and ask God to help us see new thoughts and visions clearly.

When you have to move from a peak to a valley you need to always focus on the movement and the direction and the One who always leads you safely over the next hurdle.

That's why believing is seeing.

A Taste of Goodness

Lord, Your goodness keeps us moving forward. Help me to cross through the valleys and up toward the peaks in faithfulness and joy. Amen.

No Pat Answers!

Be strong and courageous!
2 Chronicles 32:7 NLT

Life throws you a lot of curves and you can't always prepare yourself for them. Dealing with a personal crisis is hard work and takes a lot of faith to get through. What you don't need during such times is people who give you a "pat answer" for why this particular thing happened to you.

Most people have your best interests at heart and may not even recognize when they toss an old cliché your way that really isn't helping you. You know. "It happened because it's God's will!" Well, I'm not so sure. God probably spent a fair amount of time trying to direct my steps to avoid the chaos and I probably was not really listening.

When a crisis hits you, there's only one real place to go. Take it to God and ask His help. Then be strong and courageous. When life throws you a curve, just duck, because God will be right there with a catcher's mitt.

A Taste of Faithfulness
Lord, it is so wonderful to know You are always there and even in the midst of life's ups and downs, You can be counted on. Be with me today. Amen.

DECEMBER 4

A Matter of Trust

I trust in God's unfailing love forever and ever.
Psalm 52:8 NLT

You've probably learned a lot of things about trust by now and you've had to learn to look around pretty carefully and be discerning about the places you are willing to put your trust.

If you put your trust in yourself, you may be off to a good start but, believe it or not, you'll disappoint yourself in some situation and you won't be sure if you should trust yourself next time.

If you put your trust in another person, your sense of trust will break down if she fails you in a time of need.

If you put your trust in money or your job, you'll have to constantly keep protecting those things because jobs and money can be lost easily.

You have only one place to dependably put your trust. You can't look *out* for the good guys, or look *in* to figure it out yourself, you have to look *up* and let the Redeemer safeguard your heart, mind and soul.

A Taste of Trust
Lord, bless me with the fruit of Your joy and Your love. Help me to build my trust in You today. Amen.

God Almighty!

"Don't be troubled. You trust God, now trust in Me."
John 14:1 NLT

The book *Like a Mighty Wind* is full of miraculous stories. But what struck me most about the book was when the author commented on a trip he took to the United States. He said how excited he was to visit a country that believed so much in God that they even printed, "In God We Trust" on their money. He was awed by the thought and imagined all kinds of miracles that must be happening in a country that was so devoted to God. Sadly, he was shocked when he discovered that people were not as immersed in their trust of God as he had thought.

We are somewhat glib about saying we trust in God. But do we really? Only you can decide where you will place your trust and whether or not you will leave it there once you've made a choice. Trust in God. He is indeed the only sure thing in the universe.

A Taste of Peace

Lord, when I leave my life in Your hands and trust You to care for me, I am totally at peace. Help me to grow in trust. Amen.

DECEMBER 6

Right Choices! Wrong Choices!

*Oh, that you would listen to His voice
today! The LORD says, "Don't harden your hearts."*
Psalm 95:7-8 NLT

Each day we make choices and not all the choices
we make are best. Usually a wrong choice will sig-
nal you in some way. That still small voice within
you knows the difference between a wrong or a
right choice and it speaks pretty loudly when you're
heading in the wrong direction.

Erich Fromm said, "Our capacity to choose
changes constantly with our practice of life. The
longer we continue to make the wrong decisions,
the more our heart hardens; the more often we
make the right decisions, the more our heart softens
or better, perhaps, comes alive."

Let the Holy Spirit be your decision-making
guide today.

A Taste of the Spirit
Lord, I usually know if I'm making a decision that isn't
healthy or wise for myself, but I don't always have the
strength to step away from it. Please guide me in Your
love today. Amen.

Complete Trust

*May the God of hope fill you with all joy
and peace as you trust in Him.*

Romans 15:13

Since human beings are fallible, complete trust in anyone seems to be a difficult thing to achieve. What about you? Are you always there when others need you? Do you sometimes wonder if you even trust yourself?

The point is that trust is not an easy thing. We have had so little absolute trust in others and in ourselves that we even have trouble trusting God and so we are not filled with joy and peace.

What if just for an hour, you truly put your life in God's hands, totally trusting Him to guide you and protect you? When you receive the peace that passes all understanding, you'll know you've done just that. When you get there, trust God for the next hour too. It'll make a difference in everything you do.

A Taste of Trust

Lord, it is difficult to know how to trust You because we always fail in caring for each other here on earth. Please help me trust You more. Amen.

Filling Your Worry Quotient

Give all your worries and cares to God,
for He cares about what happens to you.
1 Peter 5:7 NLT

How do you handle worry? Do you worry about everything, or do you let everything just roll off your back? Most of us are somewhere in between these two. We accept worry as a sort of natural thing to do. But is it?

Covering the basics is the common point of worry. If we believe God is taking care of us, then we know the basics are covered. If we aren't sure if God is taking care of us, we're not sure anything is really covered. We hope it is, but we aren't sure.

It's time to get past your hope that God will take care of you, and believe that He is doing so even at this moment. Nothing will come into your life that will surprise Him and He will do all He can to help you with anything and everything. Sweep out the worries and relax in God's care.

A Taste of Peace
Lord, it isn't easy to step aside from worry. I always think I have to help You make things right and I know in a way I do, because I have to raise my faith and trust and believe in You. Amen.

The Last Straw

*"Don't worry about tomorrow. It will take care of itself.
You have enough to worry about today."*
Matthew 6:34 CEV

In the *Wizard of Oz*, Dorothy helps the scarecrow down from the fence and helps him pull himself together. She reminds him that he can be great and that he just needs some direction and more confidence. Even though he isn't sure he's really capable of making a decision, he follows her anyway because he has the last straw of faith.

Some of us are like that. We have allowed life's worries to become so important that we're falling apart, and we're not sure which way to go any more. We think we just aren't smart or capable enough to become what God intended us to be.

If your worries have shaken you up like that, then stuff a little more faith into your system and make your wobbly knees walk toward God. He's ready even now to renew and strengthen you.

A Taste of Faithfulness

Lord, I need Your help to get my life together now. Please meet me on the path and direct my steps toward Your will and purpose. Amen.

Losing a Little Weight

"Come to Me, all you who are weary
and burdened, and I will give you rest."
Matthew 11:28

Most of us are interested in staying as healthy as possible. We try to exercise, eat right, and do the things that will allow our bodies to operate with strength.

The same is true of your spirit. If you've been exercising your fears and worries, running on uncertainty and falling down in your prayer life, you may be out of spiritual shape. It's important to see how much your spirit weighs.

God doesn't expect you to carry more weight than you can handle. You can let go of the concerns that burden you. If you give them up, you'll feel a lot lighter. It'll be the best diet you've ever been on.

Lay those burdens at the Cross and start your day feeling lighter and brighter. You might even have dessert today because sweet peace of mind will be lifting you up.

A Taste of Faithfulness

Lord, help me to put all my cares in Your hands and to trust You to carry the weight of the world ... even my world. Amen.

Too Smart to be Wise?

Teach us to use wisely all the time we have.
Psalm 90:12 CEV

We don't seem to talk a lot these days about people who have great wisdom. We might notice those with intelligence, or business savvy, or genius IQ, but what is wisdom? Can you be too smart to be really wise? In generations passed, the great thinkers were sought out to lead and guide and offer insight to those around them. Today, we're bombarded with talkers from every direction, it's hard to know if any of them are actually brilliant, much less wise.

Proverbs 3:16-18 (CEV) uses the metaphor of an enlightened woman to describe wisdom. Wisdom provides a long life and it's one that is pleasant and safe. Wisdom provides honor and substance. Wisdom is a source of happiness, a life-giving tree. Wisdom doesn't have to have a Ph.D. It simply has to grow and stay connected to the Source of all life.

Seek Wisdom's gifts today.

A Taste of Wisdom

Lord, help me to seek Your wisdom in all that I do. Keep me ever connected to Your life-giving tree. Amen.

DECEMBER 12

A Wise Old Owl

If you love Wisdom and don't reject her,
she will watch over you.
Proverbs 4:6 CEV

It's interesting to think of wisdom as a wise old owl perched on a tree right above your house, watching what goes on and looking for opportunities to share its insights with you. A little poem by Edward Hersey Richards was written in its honor.

"A wise old owl sat on an oak,
the more he saw, the less he spoke;
the less he spoke, the more he heard:
Why aren't we like that wise old bird?"

Make today a wisdom day – listen more than you speak. Let others have the floor and respond only as you must. Listen beyond the words, beyond the situation and see if you can hear the truth in all the chatter around you. Listen the way you would hope God Himself would listen to you.

A Taste of Patience
Lord, we are always so quick to get our thoughts on the table that we're not very good at listening to those around us. Today, help me to be a thoughtful listener. Amen.

Peace from the Wild Side

The heavens declare the glory of God;
the skies proclaim the work of His hands.
Psalm 19:1

Wherever you live, you have opportunities to experience nature. Okay, some of you have to do this in a city park, but most of you can get away and enjoy creation as God intended it.

John Muir wrote, "Climb the mountains and get their good tidings. Nature's peace will flow into you as sunshine flows into trees. The winds will blow their own freshness into you, and the storms their energy, while cares will drop off like autumn leaves."

If you haven't experienced the good tidings from the mountain tops, or the freshness of the winds, then make today an opportunity to let God speak to you with clarity and power. You might be impressed with what you can learn from the sound of a winging bird or the rippling waters of a creek.

This kind of wisdom is sure to bring you peace.

A Taste of Peace
Lord, walk with me through the beauty of all You've created and speak to me in whispers that only the mountains and rivers know at every rising of the sun. Amen.

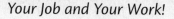
Your Job and Your Work!

Do your work willingly, as though
you were serving the Lord Himself.
Colossians 3:23 CEV

You've probably heard the old line that says, "A lot of people stop looking for work once they find a job." It's slightly humorous and sadly, somewhat truthful.

Whatever job you may have it is only part of the equation of what you're about. Your job is what you're trained to do in a specific way.

Your work is what you were born to do. You can feed those around you in heart, soul and mind through gifts of kindness, friendship and love. You can demonstrate God's love any time, any hour, any place. That's your work.

The tricky part is that God waits for you to volunteer your services. He's called you to be part of His cheering committee, but only you can do your part.

One thing is for sure, you'll never get laid off from His work.

A Taste of Faithfulness
Lord, help me to see all the work I do as something I do for You. Bless those around me and open opportunities for Your work to continue everywhere. Amen.

'Tis the Season!

"Prepare a pathway for the Lord's coming!
Make a straight road for Him!"
Matthew 3:3 NLT

During the Christmas season, church services and caroling, baking cookies and sharing time with friends all become part of the beauty, joy and the wonder of the season. Add to that the time it takes to write out your Christmas cards, remember family and friends you haven't seen all year, and you can almost wonder if it's really worth it for one special day!

It's worth it! Everything you do to commemorate our Lord's coming is worth it. At Christmas time you focus on giving, sharing and loving. You become the hands and feet of Christ. You prepare the way for Him and bring greater joy!

This year as you make room for Him to enter anew into your heart and mind, enjoy the many gifts of the season. Serve Him with joy and thanksgiving and glad tidings.

A Taste of Goodness

Lord, I am always excited at this time of year. I ask that You would inspire my heart to help anybody that I can who has not been as blessed as I have been this year. Amen.

Angel Sightings

Continue to love each other with true Christian love. Don't forget to show hospitality to strangers, for some who have done this have entertained angels without realizing it!

Hebrews 13:1-2 NLT

We seem much more aware of angels at this time of year. We sing with them and delight in the part they played in the birth of Jesus. We even hang special angel ornaments in our houses.

Angels are God's messengers on earth. We can also be messengers of goodwill and peace as we spread the news of Jesus' love for the world. We spread this message through things we do for others. Discover how you can be a messenger of goodwill this Christmas season.

You might help out in a nursing home, visit children at the hospital, visit a shut-in, or send Christmas cards to soldiers overseas.

It's nearly Christmas and it's a great time to be an angel of love and peace.

A Taste of Kindness

Lord, help me to serve those in need in any way I can throughout this holiday season. Amen.

Glad Tidings!

Suddenly, an angel of the Lord appeared among them.
"Don't be afraid!" he said. "I bring
you good news of great joy for everyone!"
Luke 2:9-10 NLT

We all love to receive good news and in the world we live in today, it seems a pretty scarce commodity indeed. It wasn't that much different for the shepherds who lived with uncertainty though. They wondered when the Redeemer would be born and restore peace and love to the world.

As we wait for the Lord's return, we have to live, work and keep waiting faithfully. We have to rest in God's love and reassure each other that good news is still ours.

As you prepare for the Christmas season, consider ways you might share good news that will bring joy to those around you. It's your chance to do the work of angels.

A Taste of Joy

Lord, we all look forward to the good news of Your saving grace and love. Help us to work and live and play with the joy of knowing Your salvation. Amen.

Christmas Child

"This very day in King David's home town a Savior was born for you. He is Christ the Lord. You will know who He is, because you will find Him dressed in baby clothes and lying on a bed of hay."

Luke 2:11-12 CEV

The Child of Christmas reaches out to the child in all of us. He reminds us that we are cradled in the arms of a God who loves us more than we can imagine. He loves us so much that He was even willing to become one of us.

As you prepare for Christmas, take some time with the infant King, the Baby born for you. The Child of Christmas embodies all the attributes sown into the seeds of the fruit of the Spirit. He is love personified, joy unmeasured, peace beyond understanding, goodness and kindness and all that is precious.

Return to the Child of Christmas and allow the child in you to see Him anew in wonder and glory.

A Taste of Goodness

Lord, bless all the children around the world this holiday season and protect them through Your grace and love. Amen.

At His Word

*The Word became a human being and lived here
with us. We saw His true glory, the glory of the only
Son of the Father. From Him all the kindness
and all the truth of God have come down to us.*

John 1:14 CEV

In Genesis we read that God spoke the world into being. As He did so, the Word was with Him. Imagine the stillness and the silence and the vast darkness until that moment when God spoke, "Let there be light."

The world was dark, hungry and lonely, and then God sent the power of the Word to create newness and the Light came into the darkness and this time it was in the form of God Himself.

As you sit quietly and watch Christmas lights twinkling around you, imagine the Word of God coming into your life to light up your heart forever. At His Word it has all come to pass.

A Taste of Kindness

Lord, what joy it brings to know that Your love lights up the universe and Your kindness fills the hearts of everyone who knows You this season. Amen.

Getting in the Spirit

*I was there and saw the Spirit come down on Him like
a dove from heaven. And the Spirit stayed on Him.*
John 1:32 CEV

Not all of us are filled with the Christmas spirit.
Why? Perhaps because we've lost the real Spirit behind the season.

Imagine being there when Jesus was baptized.
The visible Spirit of God anointed Him and was so
real even John could see it. Now imagine that same
Spirit calling your name, coming closer to you and
living in your heart and soul for all your life. If you
can imagine that, then it should be a whole lot easier for you to get into the festive mood.

The Gift of heaven lives in you and the Spirit of
all exists in and through you. Embrace His Spirit
and get out there and string some lights, make some
cookies and enjoy knowing that your spirit is totally
aligned with the most powerful and loving Spirit
that ever was and ever will be!

A Taste of Joy
Lord, I am so grateful for Your love and I thank You for
this amazing time of year and the blessings that are
mine because of You. Amen.

A Little Adoration

Shout praises to the LORD! With all my
heart I will thank the LORD when His people meet.
The LORD has done many wonderful things!
Psalm 111:1-2 CEV

Worship, praise and adoration are keys to the joys of a true Christmas celebration. Open wide the door of your heart as you embrace your friends and family and as you shine your light of love for all to see.

If you're not someone who is given to outbursts of praise and adoration to God, perhaps it's time to give in to the Spirit within you. Let your reflection of His love be seen everywhere you go. Take time alone and thank God for the blessings you've enjoyed through His grace. Take some time with others to shout adoring praises to God!

God's Gift to you was born into your heart a long time ago and it's something worthy of real celebration. Give God the glory today!

A Taste of Joy
Lord, I do give You the glory and thank You for the gifts of joy, peace and love that fill my life. I praise You, Lord, for Your immeasurable kindness to me. Amen.

Away in a Manger

Mary was engaged to Joseph and travelled with him to Bethlehem. She was soon going to have a baby, and while they were there, she gave birth to her firstborn son. She dressed Him in baby clothes and laid Him on a bed of hay, because there was no room for them in the inn.

Luke 2:5-7 CEV

It's hard to imagine as we sing the old Christmas carol, *Away in a Manger*, each year, what it really must have been like for Mary to deliver a baby in an old barn. Not only were the surroundings somewhat austere, but for a teenage girl in a strange city, having her first baby, it had to be daunting.

As you travel with Mary to Bethlehem this year, and linger with her in the stable where the baby Jesus was born, try to put yourself in her place, if only for a moment. Hers was a lesson in total trust and surrender. She committed herself to the Lord and prepared herself for the blessed event. Such honor and commitment do not necessarily mean things will be easily played out. No wonder the angels rejoiced with her.

A Taste of Goodness

Lord, You blessed Mary in a unique way and You bless each of us too. Help us find our true joy in You. Amen.

What God has Done!

*Our God has given us a mighty Savior
from the family of David His servant.*
Luke 1:69 CEV

I love the Christmas season! I love the feeling of kindness and generosity and the sense of purpose as people go about looking to find the most meaningful presents for the people they love. I love the idea of sharing and giving and peace in the world.

These day we may be more contemporary, but that doesn't mean we've lost the spirit. In fact, in recent years, I've seen more generosity during the Christmas season than I ever remember as a kid.

All of this happens for one reason. At this time of year we should thank God for the gift of our Lord and Savior and also pray that others would receive the gift of God's Son. Christmas isn't about what we do. It's about God's gift to us!

A Taste of Love

Lord, Your love for us is so incredible that You shine the brightest light possible, the star of David, the Son of the Most High, Your gift of Jesus into our lives. Thank You, Father, for loving us so much! Amen.

The Eve of Love

There were fourteen generations from Abraham to David.
There were also fourteen from David to the exile in
Babylonia and fourteen more to the birth of the Messiah.
Matthew 1:17 CEV

When Joseph learned that his young bride to be was pregnant, he wanted to quietly break off the wedding. Much to his surprise, an angel came to him in a dream and advised him to marry her after the baby was born for she was made pregnant through a miracle of the Holy Spirit.

No doubt, Joseph, like Mary, was hand-picked by God for this event. Not just any man would do. He had to be a protector and a caretaker, a man who knew how to be a loving father and husband.

As you celebrate with Mary and Joseph this holiday, honor them for their parts in bringing the baby Jesus into the world. Embrace your own family tenderly. Real love has come into the world and all of us are blessed.

A Taste of Love
Lord, thank You for Your love. Thank You for Mary and Joseph and all who helped support their lives in the raising of the baby Jesus. They have made a difference in all of our lives, even today. Amen.

Christmas Joy!

So the Lord's promise came true, just as the prophet had said, "A virgin will have a baby boy, and He will be called Immanuel," which means, "God with us."
Matthew 1:22-23 CEV

The Creator of the universe devised a miraculous plan to make it possible for His own creation to find a way back to Him. He determined to share His love by giving Himself to us in the form of a tiny baby that most naturally calls for our goodness, our generosity and our awe.

Visit the Baby and delight in His presence. Thank Him that He has come into your life and embrace His goodness. Let Him wrap His little finger around your heart in such a way that you will be attached to each other forever. Radiate joy as you think of the tiny Baby given to you as the promise of life eternal.

Let the celebration of His love remain in your heart throughout the season and throughout the year.

A Taste of Love
Lord, what joy it is to celebrate the birth of Jesus! Bless each home and each heart on this beautiful day with the gift of Your endless love. Amen.

The Wise Followers

*When Jesus was born in the village of Bethlehem
in Judea, Herod was king. During this time some
wise men from the east came to Jerusalem and said,
"Where is the Child born to be king of the Jews? We saw
His star in the east and have come to worship Him."*

Matthew 2:1-2 CEV

The men who went to worship the baby Jesus had studied the stars and the Scriptures to determine when the Christ child would be born. They were thrilled when the moment arrived and made plans to see the baby for themselves. They brought Him the most precious gifts they could find to honor Him and His family.

Today we await His return and many are studying the signs to try to determine when He might come back. Though we don't know when that will be, we do know that it is wise of us to pay attention to the times and to prepare for His coming and the day when we will be together with Him forever.

A Taste of Patience

Lord, we wait patiently and excitedly for Your return.
We look for Your star to shine in our lives and for You
to rule over the world with love. Amen.

A New Hope

*May the God of hope fill you with all joy and peace
as you trust in Him, so that you may overflow
with hope by the power of the Holy Spirit.*
Romans 15:13

A new hope was born at Christmas time. It is a living and breathing hope that can fill your heart and mind and bless your spirit. The hope of salvation and grace, the hope of promises made and kept, these are God's gifts to renew your life in Him.

As the old year winds down thank God for the special moments you enjoyed, the love you shared with friends and family and the protection and mercy He gave you each day. Wrap your memories around your heart and let them remind you of the constant hope that comes from your Redeemer.

The Holy Spirit has blessed you with Divine insight, wisdom and love this year. Trust in Him to guide you and guard you and to be ready to walk with you into a New Year. Be filled with His hope and let it overflow to those around you.

A Taste of Hope

Lord, I don't know what is ahead of me, but I thank You for sharing Your love and Your Spirit with me this past year. Let me walk in hope with You for always. Amen.

The Gift of Love

Choose to love the Lord your God and to obey Him
and to commit yourself to Him, for He is your life.
Deuteronomy 30:20 NLT

God made a commitment to you at Christmas. He sent a visible, lovable, touchable form of Himself into your life. He said, "I want you to know Me and to love Me as I love you." He did it in the best way he could imagine ... that of an innocent and tiny baby. God loves you that much.

The kind of love God has for you is an immeasurable gift. Nothing can buy it and nothing can separate you from it. You are priceless and valuable to Him.

If the fruit of the Spirit is love, then set your sights on enlarging your understanding of that beautiful fruit this year. Let God's love accompany you wherever you go, for nothing can bless your life more.

A Taste of Love

Lord, Your love is so incredible! I thank You for the gift of Jesus whose light shines in the darkness of our hearts. Bless my relationship with You and expand my love for You this coming year. Amen.

A Gift of Peace

By faith we have been made acceptable to God. And now,
because of our Lord Jesus Christ, we live at peace with God.
Romans 5:1 CEV

Visions and hopes for peace wing their way into our minds at this time of the year. The season, however, can only serve as a reminder of peace. The real possibility of peace always rests with you and with me. We must first understand what it means to truly have the kind of faith that allows us to live at peace with God. That kind of faith comes through Jesus Christ who is the Prince of Peace.

We must then apply that understanding to our daily lives and let it pour from us in all we do so others can receive it from us. We give and share our peace with them and then they pass it on as well. Peace for the world has to start with peace at home and even more so, peace within your own soul.

God has already accepted you through His Son, Jesus Christ. Let His peace reign in your heart each day of the coming year.

A Taste of Peace
Lord, thank You for accepting me and loving me as I am. Because of Jesus, grant me Your gift of peace. Amen.

The Gift of Kindness

*Christ has also introduced us to God's undeserved
kindness on which we stand. So we are happy,
as we look forward to sharing in the glory of God.*

Romans 5:2 CEV

What are gifts of kindness? Is it buying a gift for
someone's birthday or when you prepare a meal for
a family who lives in poverty? It is and it is much
more.

Most acts of kindness mean that you were inter-
acting with some of God's other children. Most of
those acts are little gifts that make your spirit lighter
and bring joy.

As the old year fades away, and the New Year
comes, remind yourself how blessed you are to live
under the kindness of God's grace. Make it a mission within your heart to share that kindness with
as many people as you possibly can.

A Taste of Kindness

Lord, as I ponder Your loving kindness to me this year,
I'm so grateful. Help me each day to share that same
kindness with those around me. Amen.

The Gift of Faithfulness

My child, don't lose sight of good planning and insight. They keep you safe on your way and keep your feet from stumbling. You can lie down without fear and enjoy pleasant dreams.
Proverbs 3:21, 23-24 NLT

As an old year ends, we look forward to the year ahead. We make plans and commitments to try again to do our best and to live godly lives. It's good to plan according to God's will and purpose. It's good to remember what God tells us in Jeremiah 29:11 (NLT) "For I know the plans I have for you," says the LORD. "They are plans for good and not for disaster, to give you a future and a hope."

Soon you'll be starting a new year. Embrace the possibility of God's goodness and His faithfulness to you. Remember to include Him in all your plans and He will keep you from stumbling and give you nights of peaceful dreams.

A Taste of Faithfulness

Lord, thank You for being with me each step of the way. Help me to walk more fully with You in the coming year. Amen.